Grievance arbitration

Grievance arbitration

A practical guide

International Labour Office   Geneva

ISBN 92-2-101722-2

First published 1977

ILO publications can be obtained through major booksellers or ILO local offices in many countries, or direct from ILO Publications, International Labour Office, CH-1211 Geneva 22, Switzerland. A catalogue or list of new publications will be sent free of charge from the above address.

Printed by Imprimerie Vaudoise, Lausanne, Switzerland

CONTENTS

INTRODUCTION

The present guide has been drawn up with a view to providing practical guidance on the establishment and operation of procedures for the settlement of workers' grievances by private arbitration.

Private arbitration of workers' grievances—that is, settlement of grievances under arbitration procedures provided for by agreement of the parties themselves—was first and most fully developed in the United States and Canada. This system of dispute settlement has been well adapted to the needs and circumstances of those countries. It is not the intention of the present guide to suggest that the system can or should be established everywhere. Indeed, it would be incompatible with the institutions and traditions of certain States. However, in recent years a growing number of governments, particularly in the developing countries, have begun to promote private arbitration as a method of settlement of grievance disputes ; those governments have apparently reached the conclusion that this method of settlement was suited to their countries' needs and conditions : the view appears to have been taken that industrial conflict arising out of workers' grievances—frequently a prime source of conflict—could be considerably diminished through private arbitration and that the resulting degree of industrial peace was important to the development effort.

In view of this growing interest in private arbitration in the developing world, it appeared to the ILO that there was a need for material to assist the establishment of such a system where it was locally desired. The present guide has been prepared for this purpose. It is addressed to government officials responsible for labour relations matters who may have to formulate policies regarding private arbitration, to employers, workers and trade union officials who may wish to make provision for grievance arbitration in the collective agreements they conclude, and to arbitrators themselves.

While specifically focused on arbitration of grievances under procedures laid down by collective agreements, certain of the indications in the present guide may also be found useful in connection with procedures before labour or industrial tribunals, where such institutions exist. In particular, Chapters IV to VI, on the parties' preparation of their cases, the arrangement and conduct of an arbitration hearing, problems of proof, and the arbitration award, may provide useful guidance to the parties to a dispute that is brought before a labour or industrial tribunal, as well as to the members of such tribunals.

The guide is largely based on North American practice, but in preparing it an effort has been made to take into account the conditions prevailing in developing countries. When using the guide the parties concerned may in any event have to adapt the suggestions made in these pages to the particular circumstances of individual countries.

The basic draft of this guide was drawn up by Mr. Arnold M. Zack, labour arbitrator in the United States. Mr. Eladio Daya and Mr. Edward Yemin of the Labour Law and Labour Relations Branch of the International Labour Office contributed to the preparation of the final version.

GRIEVANCE DISPUTES
AND THEIR SETTLEMENT

1

A "grievance dispute" needs to be clearly distinguished from other labour disputes. Moreover, private arbitration is only one of a number of means of settling such disputes, normally ensuring final settlement, as the last stage in a specified procedure for dealing with grievances. The present chapter will be devoted to elucidating these matters.

GRIEVANCE DISPUTES

In some countries no distinction is drawn, for the purpose of disputes settlement, between different types of labour disputes. In others, however, different settlement machinery is applicable to different kinds of disputes, classified according to criteria which vary from country to country. The two most prevalent types of classification distinguish rights disputes from interest (or economic) disputes and individual disputes from collective disputes. For present purposes, it is the first classification that is apposite, since grievance arbitration, as developed in practice, has been applicable essentially to rights disputes, whether involving individual or collective claims. An indication of what is usually meant by the term "grievance" is given in the Examination of Grievances Recommendation (No. 130), adopted in 1967 by the International Labour Conference, taking into account the variety of national practices. The Recommendation states that "the grounds for a grievance may be any measure or situation which concerns the relations between employer and worker or which affects or may affect the conditions of employment of one or several workers in the undertaking when that measure or situation appears contrary to provisions of an applicable collective agreement or of an individual contract of employment, to works rules, to laws or regulations or to the custom or usage of the occupation, branch of economic activity or country,

3

regard being had to principles of good faith".[1] Thus the term "grievance" is used to designate claims by workers or a trade union concerning the workers' individual or collective rights under an applicable collective agreement, individual contract of employment, law, regulation, works rules, custom or usage. Such claims involve questions relating to the interpretation or application of the rules concerned. The term "grievance" is used in certain countries to designate this type of claim, while in some other countries reference is made to disputes over "rights", or "legal" disputes.

Grievances generally arise from the day-to-day working relations in the undertaking, usually as a worker or trade union protest against an act or omission of management that is considered to violate workers' rights. Grievances typically arise on such questions as discipline and dismissal, the payment of wages and other fringe benefits, working time, overtime and time-off entitlements, promotion, demotion and transfer, rights deriving from seniority, rights of supervisors and union officers, job classification problems, the relationship of works rules to the collective agreement and the fulfilment of obligations relating to safety and health laid down in the agreement. Such grievances, if not dealt with in accordance with a procedure that secures the respect of the parties, can result in embitterment of the working relationship and a climate of industrial strife.

The principal type of grievance dealt with by grievance arbitration, and thus focused on in the present manual, consists of grievances concerning the application or interpretation of a collective agreement in force. Other types of grievances, particularly those relating to the application or interpretation of statutory provisions, are frequently settled under other procedures. Complaints of unfair dismissal, for example, which in some countries are governed by collective agreements and submitted to private arbitration, are now governed by legislation in many countries and are adjudicated by the labour tribunals.

In contrast to grievances, which are susceptible of definitive settlement on the basis of the interpretation and application of existing rules, "interest" or "economic" disputes involve differences relating to the determination of new terms and conditions of employment, in most cases originating from trade union demands or proposals concerning improvement of wages, fringe benefits, job security or other terms or conditions of employment, and most often arising in connection with the negotiation of collective agreements. Such a dispute arises if a request to negotiate is refused or if in the course of their negotiations the parties fail to reach agreement on the outstanding issues. Since there are generally no mutually binding standards that can be

---

[1] Paragraph 3. The Recommendation as a whole is reproduced in Appendix 1.

relied upon to arrive at a settlement of interest disputes and recourse must be had to bargaining power, compromise and sometimes a test of economic strength for the parties to reach an agreed solution, this type of dispute lends itself best to conciliation as a method to assist in settlement. [1] In some cases, however, the parties to such a dispute agree to submit it to binding arbitration, while in a number of countries legislation has empowered the competent authorities to refer certain interest disputes to binding arbitration, particularly in the case of disputes in essential services or disputes that if continued are likely to have an adverse effect on national health or security.

SETTLEMENT PROCEDURES IN THE PATTERN OF INDUSTRIAL RELATIONS

It is widely recognised that workers should be provided with appropriate procedures through which their grievances can be submitted and settled. This recognition is based both on considerations of fairness and justice, which require that workers' claims concerning their rights should receive fair and impartial determination, and on the desire to remove from the area of power conflict a type of dispute that can properly be settled through authoritative determination of the respective rights and obligations of the parties. Recognition of the importance of procedures for the settlement of grievances is reflected in the fact that in one form or another such procedures may be found in nearly all countries where some organised system of labour-management relations exists. It has been pointed out [2] that adequate measures for the examination of grievances are essential for the promotion and maintenance of good labour-management relations and a high degree of efficiency in the undertaking ; conversely, the lack of opportunity for workers to air their grievances and have them seriously considered tends to promote dissatisfaction and a poor level of morale among the workforce, which in turn may have a negative effect on the workers' performance at their jobs. Moreover, effective grievance procedures facilitate communication to management of difficulties within the undertaking which might require remedial measures on the part of management. Furthermore, by contributing to the creation of a climate of mutual confidence and respect, such procedures help to establish a relationship between the parties which enhances the prospects of the harmonious functioning of collective bargaining itself. Some experts

---

[1] In this connection see ILO : *Conciliation in industrial disputes,* a practical guide (Geneva, 1973).

[2] ILO : *Examination of grievances and communications within the undertaking,* Report VII (1), International Labour Conference, 50th Session, Geneva, 1966, pp. 8-9.

even feel that grievance procedures should be regarded as an essential component of any effective system of application of a collective agreement.

In addition to enhancing the prospects of industrial peace by providing an established procedure for hearing one type of worker protest, grievance procedures constitute in certain systems a substitute for, or a delaying factor in respect of, direct action in the form of strikes : this is the case, for example, in countries in which strikes are prohibited, under legislation or collective agreements or in practice, during the term of a collective agreement, and the parties are obliged to submit any dispute concerning its application or interpretation to the grievance procedure.

The importance of the existence of a procedure for the settlement of workers' grievances was recognised by the International Labour Conference in adopting the Examination of Grievances Recommendation, 1967 (No. 130). Paragraph 2 of that Recommendation provides that "any worker who, acting individually or jointly with other workers, considers that he has grounds for a grievance should have the right (*a*) to submit such grievance without suffering any prejudice whatsoever as a result, and (*b*) to have such grievance examined pursuant to an appropriate procedure". According to Paragraph 5 of the Recommendation, the parties to collective agreements establishing grievance procedures should be encouraged to undertake in the agreement to promote settlement of grievances under the procedures provided for, and to abstain from any action which might impede the effective functioning of these procedures.

Under most grievance procedures established by collective agreement, claims concerning rights under the agreement may be made by the workers but not by the employer. This is quite understandable : on substantive matters, collective agreements mainly establish certain rights of the worker and obligations of the employer ; complaints concerning violation of the terms of an agreement thus necessarily relate principally to employers' acts or omissions. Also, to the extent that workers have certain obligations under an agreement, those obligations can be enforced by employers through the exercise of their disciplinary authority. Because workers have no similar power, they have to rely on a grievance procedure, or otherwise on strike action, to ensure respect for their rights and protection against abuse of the management's disciplinary authority.

SETTLEMENT WITHIN THE UNDERTAKING

Grievance procedures may be divided roughly into two categories : those applicable within the undertaking and those applicable outside the undertaking, which include arbitration.[1] Where grievance procedures are laid down in collective agreements, both types are frequently provided for, those of the second type being resorted to after the first have been exhausted. Recommendation No. 130 contains guidelines with respect to both types of grievance procedure.

Procedures for the settlement of grievances within the undertaking are most frequently established by collective agreement or by unilateral employer action in works rules. However, they are sometimes established pursuant to legislation, or to general agreements between central organisations of employers and workers. If a grievance procedure within an undertaking is to fulfil its function effectively, it is essential that the workers should be familiar with it; they should have confidence in the fairness of the management in handling grievances and should not suffer reprisals for presenting them; the procedure must also be expeditious.

In large undertakings, a common type of grievance procedure involves successive steps at different levels, a worker's grievance being first discussed with the immediate supervisor, and then if no solution is found with higher levels of management. The number of levels and steps in the procedure usually increases with the size of the undertaking. Sometimes, when an important question of principle which would involve a number of workers is concerned the matter may go directly to a higher level of management. Under some procedures, bipartite or joint grievance committees within the undertaking, composed of representatives of management and workers, hear grievances when they have been considered at lower levels at a number of earlier stages in the procedure. A settlement reached jointly by the worker and management representatives at any level is generally regarded as final and binding on the parties. A grievance is also deemed to be settled if an appeal is not lodged at the next highest level within a given time.

The consideration of a grievance through the grievance procedure will usually take the form of informal discussions or negotiations, although it may also take the form of an investigation or hearing. In some countries the handling of grievances is indistinguishable in practice from the usual procedure followed in negotiating agreements, which is also applied to negotiating a solution to a grievance. Workers' representatives frequently participate in the grievance procedure within the undertaking by advising workers on the nature and extent of their rights, assisting workers in presenting their grievances to management and representing the workers concerned at different steps in the procedure. Depending upon the national system, workers'

---

[1] Indications regarding both types of procedures are given in *Examination of grievances and communications within the undertaking,* op. cit.

representatives may be shop stewards or trade union officials or staff delegates elected by the workers in the undertaking. Sometimes works councils or similar bodies within the undertaking composed of workers' representatives are competent to deal with workers' grievances.

SETTLEMENT OUTSIDE THE UNDERTAKING

When grievances are not satisfactorily settled within the undertaking, they may give rise to an atmosphere of tension and conflict affecting worker-management relations and the efficiency of work, and may result in confrontation and disruption of production.

In many countries there is provision, by law or collective agreement, for submission of such disputes to final settlement outside the undertaking. Procedures laid down by law generally involve submission of grievance disputes to special labour tribunals or to the ordinary courts. Where the matter is covered by collective agreements, it is usually laid down that the dispute should be referred to the decision of an arbitrator or arbitrators chosen by the parties. However, legislation also may in some cases provide for submission of certain types of grievance disputes to private arbitration, while collective agreements may provide for the determination of disputes concerning their application or interpretation by the courts or tribunals.

In some countries an appeal to the ordinary courts is the only possibility available to workers to have their grievances finally determined by an impartial body outside the undertaking—particularly grievances arising out of labour legislation, collective agreements and the contract of employment. However, it has often been found that the ordinary courts are inappropriate for dealing with many questions arising in connection with such grievances. In the first place, proceedings before such courts are often too complex, formalistic, lengthy and costly. Secondly it has often been found that such courts do not know enough about labour relations and follow rules of interpretation and of evidence that are inappropriate in that context. As a result, ordinary courts have often failed to attract the confidence of the parties to labour disputes, who have preferred to settle their disputes outside the ordinary court system. Owing to the above-mentioned shortcomings of the ordinary courts in dealing with labour disputes, an increasing number of countries have set up special labour courts or tribunals, sometimes called industrial or arbitration tribunals, to hear and dispose of industrial disputes, including grievance disputes. Such tribunals may be composed of equal numbers of representatives of workers and employers (sometimes with an independent chairman) or entirely of independent persons with a knowledge of labour relations. Proceedings before such tribunals are less formal and less costly or without cost, and are generally more expeditious, although in practice considerable backlogs of cases may develop in labour tribunals as well. Moreover, because these tribunals are part of the judicial system or are invested with appropriate powers, they are able to adjudicate rights disputes with authority and finality.

Another procedure, which has been followed in a growing number of countries, is private grievance arbitration, i.e. arbitration provided for by a collective agreement and usually applicable only to disputes concerning the interpretation or application of the collective agreement. This type of procedure can be found in countries that have not set up labour tribunals, as well as in certain countries that have. Indeed in certain countries, as will be seen in the next chapter, inclusion in collective agreements of clauses providing for private grievance arbitration has been made mandatory by legislation. In these cases, in which the collective agreement lays down a procedure for the initial examination of grievances within the undertaking and for final settlement by arbitration, the agreement may be considered to be the law of the undertaking or industry to which it applies, and to be supplemented by a kind of private judiciary set up by the parties themselves for the application and interpretation of the agreement. The initial grievance procedure is designed to filter the number of grievances and settle the minor and less difficult grievances within the undertaking, thereby reducing the number of disputes submitted to final settlement by outside arbitration. [1]

PRIVATE ARBITRATION AS A METHOD OF SETTLEMENT OF GRIEVANCES

Private arbitration of workers' grievances may be described as a method of settlement of grievance disputes through the determination of a person or persons, pursuant to an agreement between the parties to the dispute. Arbitration procedures imposed by law, and requiring the determination of disputes by bodies specified by law, may be assimilated to labour court procedures, which are not dealt with in the present manual ; on the other hand systems under which the parties to a collective agreement are merely obliged by law to include provision for grievance arbitration in the agreement, and which thus allow the parties to decide themselves who will arbitrate such disputes, will be considered to be private arbitration for present purposes.

While it is possible for private arbitration to be made applicable to all grievance disputes, including those arising under legislation as well as those

---

[1] An example of a grievance procedure ending in arbitration is given in Appendix 2.

arising under a collective agreement, in practice collective agreements with provisions for arbitration of grievances generally limit such arbitration to disputes regarding the interpretation or application of the agreement itself. (Enforcement and interpretation of legislation is ordinarily left to the established court system, which may or may not include labour tribunals, or to quasi-judicial bodies.)

Private arbitration as a method of settling grievances is of growing significance. First developed in several industrialised countries during and since the Second World War, it has become of growing interest to a number of developing countries in recent years. The reasons for this are not difficult to understand. Certain recent developments in conditions of work and labour-management relations, including the administration of agreements, increase the possibilities of differences and disputes, particularly in larger enterprises. Provision for final settlement of such disputes at the level at which they occur limits the burden placed on the ordinary courts or (where they exist) the labour tribunals, which tend to be quickly overloaded if all labour disputes are submitted to them for settlement. By relieving ordinary courts or labour tribunals of some of their burden, particularly in regard to minor grievance disputes, and by providing for expeditious adjudication of disputes at the level of the enterprise or industry, thereby avoiding the adverse effects on the industrial relations system resulting from delays in disposing of these cases, private arbitration can make a substantial contribution to the maintenance of good labour relations.

Since it is established by the parties themselves, the private arbitration of grievance disputes has the particular advantage of bringing the dispute settlement procedure down to the level of the parties to disputes. Workers and management tend to have greater confidence in a settlement machinery which is in effect their own. Also, since such arbitration is established by agreement, it is more flexible than other procedures and can be adjusted to the views, desires and experience of the parties and to the circumstances of the undertaking or industry. Moreover this procedure, operating on the level closest to the parties to disputes, has the advantage of enabling the arbitrators to acquire a much greater familiarity with the characteristics of the particular undertaking or industry concerned than most courts or tribunals. The procedure is relatively expeditious when compared with that of ordinary courts or labour tribunals ; it is informal in character ; and on that account as well as because the disputes are handled by the parties themselves often without recourse to outside lawyers, it tends to be less expensive than other procedures (although where the fees of the arbitrator must be paid by the parties, a matter to be discussed later, the costs may be somewhat more than in labour tribunals).

The private arbitration of grievances has a further advantage which should be recalled. Agreements making provision for it frequently also contain an undertaking that the trade union and workers will refrain from strike action and the employer from lockouts during the course of the agreement in matters concerning the application or interpretation of the agreement ; sometimes this undertaking extends to strikes or lockouts of any type while the agreement is in force. It is an important characteristic of such agreements that they ensure a large measure of industrial peace while they are in force. In such cases, acceptance by the employer of binding third-party arbitration of grievances may be considered to be the quid pro quo for acceptance by the trade union and workers of limitations on the right to strike.

This kind of grievance arbitration generally entails final and binding determination of the disputes submitted to the procedure. Indeed, a number of the principal advantages of this procedure would be lost if appeal to the courts or tribunals were allowed as a matter of course. This is why certain national laws or court decisions interpreting the legislation have laid down that if the parties intended in their agreement to provide for final settlement by arbitration that intention is to be respected, and appeal from arbitration awards should be allowable only in very exceptional cases. The grounds for appeal may vary, being limited for example to abuse of authority and gross incompetence,[1] or to cases in which the award was procured by corruption, fraud or other improper means or was based on partiality or corruption of the arbitrator or on failure to provide either party with a fair and impartial hearing, or in which the arbitrator exceeded his power or exercised it so imperfectly that a definite, final and mutually binding award was not made.[2]

Although private arbitration has distinct advantages when compared to proceedings in ordinary courts or labour tribunals as a method of settling grievance disputes, not every country nor every undertaking may find it possible to institute this system. In the first place, the introduction of private arbitration of grievance disputes presupposes that the State is willing to leave the settlement of such disputes to procedures decided upon by the parties themselves. In countries with a tradition of extensive state intervention in such matters, where the dispute settlement function is entirely pre-empted by government bodies, the development of private grievance arbitra-

---

[1] Philippines Labor Code, 1974, section 262. See ILO : *Legislative Series* (subsequently cited as *LS*), 1974—Phi. 1A.

[2] Provisions contained in many state arbitration statutes in the United States. See A. P. Blockhaus : *Grievance arbitration case studies* (Boston, Massachusetts, Cahners, 1974), p. 5.

tion may be difficult. Apart from a public policy favourable to private procedures for dispute settlement, two further conditions appear to be necessary for such arbitration to be successful. First, it would appear that this system is more easily instituted by undertakings over a minimum size, or by groups of smaller undertakings that together accept by agreement such a procedure for settling disputes concerning the application or interpretation of agreements covering the individual undertakings or the group as a whole. Secondly, it is difficult for grievance arbitration to function successfully in the absence of strong trade unions able to advise and assist individual workers and groups of workers in presenting their grievances and to share the costs of the procedure with the employer or employers.

PROMOTION OF PRIVATE ARBITRATION

2

VOLUNTARY AND COMPULSORY SYSTEMS

The development of an appropriate system for the settlement of workers' grievances through private arbitration presupposes a policy judgement that claims or disputes of this nature are properly made subject to a procedure, established by the parties themselves, for final and impartial determination of their rights and obligations. Such a judgement is based on the general proposition that disputes concerning rights and obligations should not be resolved by power conflict but by impartial third-party decision, supplemented by the view that the third-party procedures for the settlement of disputes concerning the interpretation and application of collective agreements in the labour field are best established by agreement of the parties themselves. In some countries this judgement has been left entirely to the parties to make. In certain others, it has become a matter of public policy, applied through administrative action or through legislation.

PROMOTION BY THE PUBLIC AUTHORITIES

Where the promotion of the private arbitration of grievance disputes is a matter of public policy, the government may confine itself to encouragement, in which case private arbitration remains entirely a voluntary procedure decided upon by the parties. In other countries legislation has been adopted obliging the parties to include in their collective agreements provision for final settlement of grievances, in which case one may speak of compulsory arbitration (although the parties may remain free to opt in their agreement for whatever particular arbitration procedure they may prefer).

The first legislation to promote the private arbitration of grievance disputes was adopted in North America, where the practice of including arbitration clauses in collective agreements grew in the years preceding the Second World War and became obligatory under legislation or administrative decisions adopted during that war. The promotion of such arbitration continued in both the United States and Canada after the war was over. In the United States, when the National Labor Relations Act of 1935 was amended in 1947 and a federal mediation and conciliation service was established, the amending Act provided that mediation and conciliation services were to be made available in the case of grievance disputes only as a last resort : "final adjustment by a method agreed upon by the parties" was declared "to be the desirable method for settlement of grievance disputes arising over the application or interpretation of an existing collective bargaining agreement". [1] Some 90 per cent of major agreements in the United States contain provision for grievance arbitration by private arbitrators. [2] In Canada the Dominion Industrial Relations and Disputes Investigation Act, 1948 (which superseded the wartime legislation), carried into the postwar era the obligation to include provision for settling grievance disputes in collective agreements. This provision, variations of which may be found in the legislation of most of the provinces, is as follows :

> Every collective agreement shall contain a provision for final settlement without stoppage of work, by arbitration or otherwise, of all differences between the parties to or employees bound by the collective agreement, concerning its interpretation, application, administration or alleged violation. [3]

Reference may be made in this connection also to New Zealand, where the Industrial Relations Act, 1973, requires that each collective agreement (as well as industrial awards which in New Zealand may take the place of collective agreements) must contain provision "for the final and conclusive settlement, without stoppage of work, of all disputes of rights, including differences between the persons bound by the award or agreement concerning its interpretation, application or operation". [4] The legislation sets forth the terms of the clause which must be included in collective agreements and awards ; this clause provides for arbitration by a tripartite committee, with final appeal to an industrial court.

Apart from the industrialised or developed countries, certain developing countries have included provisions in their labour relations legislation making inclusion of arbitration clauses in collective agreements mandatory. These countries have apparently considered that settlement of disputes regarding the application and interpretation of collective agreements pursuant to a procedure agreed upon by the parties could contribute significantly to the estab-

---

[1] Labor-Management Relations Act, 1947 (*LS* 1947—USA 2), section 203 *(d)*.

[2] See United States Department of Labor, Bureau of Labor Statistics : *Characteristics of major collective bargaining agreements, July 1, 1974*, Bulletin 1880 (1975), p. 77.

[3] Now contained in section 155 of the Canada Labour Code.

[4] Industrial Relations Act, 1973 (*LS* 1973—NZ 1), sections 115-116.

lishment of the degree of industrial peace that many have felt to be essential for development policies to be effectively carried out. In Ghana, for example, the Industrial Relations Act, 1965, provides as follows :

Every collective agreement under this Act shall contain a provision for final and conclusive settlement, by arbitration or otherwise, of all differences between the persons to whom the agreement applies concerning its interpretation. [1]

In the Philippines, the Labor Code of 1974 provides as follows :

Art. 260. *Administration of agreements.* The parties to a collective bargaining shall include in their agreement provisions to [e]nsure mutual observance of the terms and conditions of the agreement and to establish a machinery for the adjustment of grievances.

Art. 261. *Grievances machinery.* All disputes, grievances or matters arising from the implementation or interpretation of a collective bargaining agreement shall be threshed out in accordance with the grievance procedure provided by such agreement.

Art. 262. *Voluntary arbitration.* Disputes, grievances or matters not settled through the grievance procedure shall be referred to and decided or settled through the prescribed voluntary arbitration procedure in the collective bargaining agreement.

Every collective bargaining agreement shall designate in advance an arbitrator or panel of arbitrators or include a provision making the selection of such arbitrator or panel of arbitrators definite and certain when the need arises. Such arbitrator or panel of arbitrators shall have exclusive and original jurisdiction to settle or decide all disputes, grievances, or matters arising from the implementation or interpretation of a collective bargaining agreement after going through the grievance procedure. ...

Voluntary arbitration awards or decisions shall be final, unappealable and executory. ... [2]

Other countries have also provided for grievance or dispute settlement procedures to be included in collective agreements, without requiring that such procedures terminate in arbitration. This is the case, for example, in Jamaica, Malaysia, Panama and Zambia. [3] In Jamaica disputes not settled pursuant to such procedures are referred to government conciliation and with the agreement of the parties to an industrial tribunal. In Malaysia the legislation requires the parties to prescribe a procedure for "the adjustment of any question that may arise as to the implementation or interpretation" of collective agreements, ending with final reference to an industrial court.

Where inclusion of final settlement procedures in collective agreements is obligatory, different means of enforcing that obligation have been laid down. In Canada, for example, if a collective agreement does not contain

---

[1] Industrial Relations Act, 1965 (*LS* 1965—Ghana 2), section 12.

[2] Labor Code (*LS* 1974—Phi. 1A).

[3] See Jamaica, Labour Relations and Industrial Disputes Act, 1975, section 6 ; Malaysia, Industrial Relations Act, 1967 (*LS* 1967—Mal. 1A), section 13 ; Panama, Labour Code (*LS* 1971—Pan. 1), section 403 ; Zambia, Industrial Relations Act, 1971 (*LS* 1971—Zam. 2), section 112.

a provision for final settlement, a labour relations board is required, on request by either party to the agreement, to furnish such a provision, which is then deemed to be part of the agreement and binding on the parties and employees covered by the agreement. In New Zealand, a detailed procedure for settlement of this type of dispute is included in every collective agreement by operation of law, and accordingly the question of enforcement does not arise.

PROMOTION BY OTHER BODIES

Grievance arbitration may sometimes be promoted not by the public authorities but by an agreement or declaration of central organisations of employers and workers or a decision of a national tripartite labour body or conference. Such agreements or declarations may also be useful to supplement legislation on the subject. The Cyprus Basic Agreement of 1962, for instance, establishes standard rules for settlement of grievances over the interpretation or implementation of existing collective agreements. According to those rules, unresolved disputes must be submitted to arbitration by arbitrators appointed by the parties concerned or, failing agreement, by the Minister of Labour and Social Insurance ; the arbitration awards are considered final and morally binding. In Fiji, the Industrial Relations Code of Practice establishes procedures for dealing with individual grievances as well as collective disputes, including collective rights disputes concerning the application or interpretation of existing collective agreements or contracts of employment, and provides that "arbitration by independent arbitrators is particularly suitable for settling disputes of right, and its wider use for that purpose is desirable. Where it is used voluntarily the parties are bound by the award." In the Philippines, the Voluntary Code of Principles on Labor-Management Relations, adopted by the Manila Regional Labor Conference on 19 September 1956, provides that "management and labor, being in agreement on the desirability and soundness of voluntary arbitration in the settlement of disputes concerning the interpretation, implementation and enforcement of a contract during its life, shall endeavor to encourage the development and use of arbitration facilities".

ADMINISTRATION AND SERVICING

If grievance arbitration is to be promoted, there will need to be enough qualified arbitrators, and the parties may need to be helped to choose one who will meet their requirements. These functions should normally fall on the government services responsible for industrial relations or conciliation.

The main task involved is to seek out potentially qualified arbitrators and prepare a roster of suitable candidates. The administering agency may also engage in other promotional activities, such as preparing model agreements on grievance procedures and grievance arbitration, establishing rules for arbitration procedure, organising or assisting in the training of potential arbitrators and of management and trade union representatives, and reviewing past experience to find ways of overcoming difficulties and improving the process. In some countries it may be possible for these tasks, or certain of them, to be assumed by private non-profit organisations, either instead of or in addition to the government services. Such private organisations may, for example, take on the function of developing an adequate supply of trained arbitrators or suggest suitable arbitrators for particular cases. There may be advantages in bringing together employers' and workers' organisations in such a private organisation, for the joint development of arbitration facilities. Alternatively, such organisations may be brought into being by tripartite action of employers' and workers' organisations and the government, or by arbitrators themselves.

QUALIFICATIONS OF ARBITRATORS

If a system of grievance arbitration is to be successful, the arbitrators must have the qualifications to ensure that the parties will entrust them with the responsibility for making decisions on the questions at issue. Arbitrators should have an understanding of the complexities of the labour-management relationship. They should have a knowledge of collective bargaining and the operation of grievance procedures, as well as skill and experience in the interpretation of collective agreements, and familiarity with personnel policies, industrial discipline and human relations. In addition, potential arbitrators must be persons of manifest integrity. Theirs should be a non-partisan professional position and they should have a deep sense of impartiality, which requires that they should be free from commitment to, or prejudice in favour of, one side or the other. They must also be committed to the maintenance of harmonious labour-management relations, and have a strong belief in the importance of successful grievance arbitration.

Another very important qualification of potentially qualified persons is that they must be acceptable to the parties. Acceptability in this sense is an indeterminate quality, which may be related to personality and which leads the parties to agree on one individual rather than another. A party to a dispute may find an arbitrator unacceptable if that party considers the arbitrator to favour the other side or to be lacking in practical experience, or if the arbitrator fails to give an impression of responsibility and mature judgement. Acceptability is, of course, an essential attribute in the case of voluntary and private grievance arbitration. The success of this system depends on the willingness of the parties to agree to the procedure and be bound by its results.

AVAILABILITY OF QUALIFIED ARBITRATORS

It may be particularly difficult to find qualified arbitrators in the early stages of the promotion of grievance arbitration. Initially, it is necessary to seek out persons with appropriate qualifications, to develop their interest in arbitration and to establish procedures by which the parties will become aware of their availability and be induced to use their services. In some developing countries there will be few individuals with enough experience or expertise in industrial dispute resolution who also have a neutral standing: most of those who have acquired this kind of experience have served as advocates for either labour or management in their capacity as trade union officers or personnel managers respectively. However, there may be a few such persons with labour or management backgrounds who have shown sufficient objectivity to be held in high regard by both parties and to be acceptable to both as arbitrators. In view of the limited number of such individuals, potential arbitrators will also have to be sought in other fields and their availability made known to the parties. This is particularly important where awareness of the existence of available arbitrators might stimulate the parties into more extensive use of the process. The legal profession and government service are two fertile areas where qualified persons may be found, particularly among those who have acquired reputations for integrity and capability. Those who come from the government service, including retired public servants, may have the additional value of having acquired some experience of industrial problems through work in conciliation services, or in departments of labour or economic development, which might increase the appeal of such individuals to both sides.

In addition to practising lawyers and government officials, other potential arbitrators may be found in educational institutions, particularly among teachers of law, industrial relations, economics, business, psychology or other disciplines, who are familiar with the industrial life of the nation. Such faculty members may have played an active part in economic development or in the study of industrial relations. Although such individuals may not have had the practical experience of working directly with labour or management, their academic experience and their continuing contacts with the parties might suit them for the role of arbitrator. The same may be said of civic leaders, the clergy and persons in other fields such as engineering, where their daily activity may bring them into contact with the parties.

It would be desirable to draw up a roster of persons having the requisite background, qualifications and experience, for communication to the parties interested in using arbitration. To establish such a roster information on potential arbitrators must be collected, testimonials as to their acceptability obtained, certifying as to their qualifications, and the parties must be assisted in making their designation. Such a roster could be established from nominations of potential arbitrators by labour and management ; once nominations were received, it might be desirable to inquire whether the nominations of one side were genuinely acceptable to the other. As mentioned before, all these tasks might be performed by the labour relations division or the conciliation service in the department of labour ; recourse might also be had to the industrial court or to any other suitable government agency.

TRAINING

In countries where arbitration is a novelty and skilled arbitrators are few if available at all, special training could help potential arbitrators to carry out their future tasks efficiently. Satisfactory participation in a training course could be a qualification for listing on the roster of qualified arbitrators drawn up by the competent body. The training could cover industrial relations in general, basic contractual and legal principles, problems likely to be encountered in arbitration practice, and the techniques of running an arbitration hearing and writing arbitration awards where written awards are required. The course could consist of lectures, mock arbitration proceedings and informal seminars.

People who have actually served as arbitrators could speak of their experiences. University professors could lecture on such subjects as economics, industrial relations and national development. Management and trade union officials could describe existing industrial relations practices and problems. Government officials could describe the relationship of arbitration to government-provided conciliation services, as well as indicate the effect of labour and other legislation on arbitration and the arbitration award. It might prove to be valuable to bring one or more practising arbitrators from some other countries which have had greater arbitration experience to provide insights into some of the problems of arbitration. The training could give emphasis to the unique aspects of the structure surrounding arbitration practice in the particular country, adapting universal arbitration practice and procedures to those conditions.

It would also be advisable to provide for the training of management and trade union representatives. Their training should be wider in scope, including both grievance procedures and grievance arbitration. In many developing countries there are well established employers' and workers' organisations which can organise training for their respective sides, but it would also be useful to organise a training course for the two sides, in which the government administering agency can take the initiative or provide support. The most effective results can probably be achieved through co-ordinated training programmes. For example, at the time of the arbitrators' training course, two parallel courses could be run for management and trade union officials. For some subjects the same training material could be used, and the three groups could be brought together in joint lectures, symposia and discussions. At the conclusion of the three training courses, the groups could combine for mock arbitration sessions, and for a course critique and general discussions of their respective problems and outlook. This merged session would give management and trade union people an opportunity to meet the available arbitrators, and perhaps to assess their abilities. It would also enable the potential arbitrators to establish contact with the representatives of labour and management who would make use of their services.

COSTS OF PROCEEDINGS

In grievance arbitration the costs, if any, are borne by the parties, the common costs being usually shared equally between them. Where these costs include an arbitrator's fee (a per diem charge plus travel and living expenses where necessary), this fee is a major item in the total cost to be borne by the parties and may present a serious problem in many developing countries. Only unions with sufficient financial resources can afford to pay their share of the costs, and the number of such unions may be very small. If one or both of the parties cannot afford to pay the costs, it may be possible to establish a special roster of qualified arbitrators willing to serve free of charge as a service to the community. They might include retired judges, government officials, university professors and other persons with a sufficient regular income. They may also include serving judges, government officials and state university professors, under arrangements by which they can devote part of their time to arbitration work without loss of pay and benefits. Consideration might also be given to partial financing out of public funds or by central organisations of employers and workers.

THE ARBITRATION AGREEMENT

3

One of the first decisions the parties must take in the case of voluntary arbitration is whether to agree in advance to arbitration of future grievances or to agree to arbitration only after a grievance has arisen in respect of that particular grievance.

TYPES OF AGREEMENTS

In countries having some experience with grievance arbitration, provision for arbitration is usually included in the collective agreement as the last step in a comprehensive grievance procedure beginning with attempted settlement within the undertaking. The agreement to go to arbitration is thus contained in a provision intended to govern the relations between the parties over a certain time, and consists of an agreement to submit to arbitration all grievances arising during that period.

The conclusion of ad hoc agreements which have to be made each time a grievance dispute arises tends to be much less effective, since a party may resist agreeing to arbitration if it is not sure of its case. It is generally preferable to have advance agreement providing for arbitration of all disputes arising during the currency of the agreement, before a particular dispute comes into focus. This blanket advance commitment to rely on arbitration for the final settlement of grievance disputes establishes a foreseeable pattern of conduct for the parties ; it obviates procedural differences between the parties which might arise over any individual grievance and contributes to the stability of their relationship. As experience with the process grows, there should be increasing realisation of its psychological and remedial value to the parties as well as to individual workers, and of its importance as a practical substitute for the economic pressure of a strike or lockout.

Arbitration of future grievance disputes may be provided for under different types of collective agreement. One of these types is the comprehensive collective agreement : in addition to provisions concerning terms and conditions of employment and possibly other matters, such an agreement also lays down rules and procedures governing relations between the parties, including a grievance procedure culminating in arbitration. Grievance arbitration has had its greatest development under this type of agreement. Another, more limited type of collective agreement is the recognition agreement, also between an employer and a trade union : such an agreement provides for the recognition of the trade union as the collective bargaining representative of the workers concerned, and may also establish procedures for dealing with different types of problems or matters, such as the negotiation of collective agreements, the settlement of interest disputes and joint consultation, as well as the settlement of grievances through arbitration. Still another type of collective agreement providing for a sort of grievance arbitration is that between employers' and workers' organisations in general or in a particular industry or occupation, concerning the prevention and settlement of disputes or the establishment of joint conciliation and arbitration machinery.

ENTITLEMENT TO SUBMIT DISPUTES TO ARBITRATION

Another question which arises is who should be entitled to demand arbitration. Since grievances are generally regarded in collective arrangements as being workers' complaints (few grievance procedures cover employer complaints as well), it might be thought that it is only the workers' side that could submit a grievance to arbitration. This is so under many agreements, but others authorise either party to bring an unsettled grievance dispute to arbitration.

A more difficult question concerns whether, on the workers' side, it is the trade union or the individual worker that may ask for arbitration. Since the parties to the agreement are the trade union and the employer (although the individual workers are also bound by the agreement), the union or the employer would ordinarily be responsible for initiating proceedings to settle differences regarding the interpretation or application of the agreement. Accordingly, under many agreements the trade union may submit unresolved grievances to arbitration. However, under some either the union or the worker, or only the individual worker concerned, is authorised to do so. If this right is restricted to the trade union, the grievances submitted to arbitration will be filtered by a party having some interest in limiting use of the procedure to disputes that have some foundation and importance. Such a restriction tends to reinforce the position of the trade union, since its monopoly over submission of grievances to arbitration acts as an incentive for workers to join the union concerned and maintain their membership in good standing. Also it ensures that the parties most able to bear the costs of the procedure have some control over its use.

On the other hand it is essential that the rights of the individual worker be adequately safeguarded ; if individual workers are unable to have a grievance they consider well founded submitted to some method of impartial and final determination, they may be unable to have their rights respected. While in the great majority of cases the trade union may be expected to submit to arbitration all unresolved grievances having some foundation, there are cases in which the union may not do so for reasons unrelated to the merits. For example, workers in an undertaking who are not members of the union as well as union members who for one reason or another have antagonised the union leaders may have difficulty in prevailing on the union to put forward their grievances. Other workers may suffer discriminatory treatment on grounds other than union membership. For these reasons, trade unions in some countries are under an obligation to represent fairly all workers covered by the relevant collective agreement. If the individual worker as well as the union has the right to go to arbitration, the problem of payment of costs arises. Sometimes the costs are divided between the employer and the trade union if the worker has won the case (on the ground that the trade union should have brought the case on the worker's behalf but failed to do so), while a worker who loses must bear the part of the costs ordinarily assumed by the union. This acts as a disincentive for a worker to bring frivolous grievances to arbitration.

There remains the question of the role of minority unions in grievance arbitration in systems providing exclusive bargaining rights for the union with the largest membership in a bargaining unit. Generally it appears that the union entitled to conclude a collective agreement on behalf of all workers in a given bargaining unit is alone entitled to use the grievance arbitration procedure provided for in the agreement. However, in some cases the minority union may retain the right to do so on behalf of its members or may be entitled to assist or represent members who themselves have the right to make use of the procedure.

SCOPE OF ARBITRATION

Where a system of voluntary arbitration is operative, only the issues that have been agreed upon by the parties as arbitrable can be submitted to arbitration under the agreement. Conceivably the parties could agree to coverage so broad as to embrace any and all disputes between the parties ; almost always, however, the parties limit their use of arbitration to questions concerning the application or interpretation of the provisions of the applicable collective agreement. Such a limitation is achieved by a provision along the following lines :

■ Any grievance concerning the interpretation or application of this agreement shall be submitted to arbitration at the request of the aggrieved party if it has not been satisfactorily settled through the procedure outlined above [the grievance procedure within the undertaking].

The agreement may also specify questions that shall not be subject to arbitration (such as certain management prerogatives), or it may otherwise limit the scope of the arbitrator's authority. The scope of arbitration is a matter for negotiation between the parties, and the arbitrator they designate is consequently bound by the terms of their agreement. Some agreements make this limitation explicit by including a clause such as the following :

■ The arbitrator shall have no power to add to, subtract from, alter or otherwise change or modify the terms and conditions of this agreement, but shall be authorised only to interpret the existing provisions of the agreement and apply them to the specific facts of the grievance or dispute.

Whether any particular issue is arbitrable is generally initially decided by the arbitrator himself as a question separate from the merits of the substantive issue involved. This is usually done by the arbitrator on the ground that arbitrability is itself an issue for arbitration within the meaning of the arbitration clause ; and indeed the parties' agreement may so specify. It is far less costly and time-consuming than having that preliminary issue settled by the courts. If the respondent questions the arbitrability of an issue, the arbitrator will usually hear the arguments on both arbitrability and the merits of the issue at the same sitting, reserving judgement on arbitrability while hearing the merits to save the parties the need for calling a second hearing. Thus he will have sufficient information to make his decision on the merits if he finds an issue to be arbitrable. Some arbitrators, on the other hand, may refuse to hear arguments on the merits until they have ruled on arbitrability.

The courts may become involved with questions of arbitrability in certain circumstances. For example, under the legal systems of Canada, the United States and certain other countries, one party may bring an action for an injunction to prevent the other from proceeding to arbitration or to prevent the arbitrator from hearing the case either on the arbitrability issue or on the merits. As previously indicated, initial recourse to the courts on the arbitrability issue is usually more costly and time-consuming than permitting the arbitrator to decide the issue in the first instance. Arbitrability may also come to the attention of the court after the arbitrator has issued an award, if enforcement of the award is sought in the courts. Here the courts may deem the arbitrability issue to have been waived at the time of arbitration, unless when arbitrating on the merits the party concerned reserved its right to challenge arbitrability later.

SINGLE ARBITRATORS OR BOARDS

The responsibility for arbitrating a grievance may be assigned by the parties to the agreement to a single arbitrator or to an arbitration board. If only one arbitrator is named, that person must clearly have the confidence of both sides. The possible difficulty of achieving agreement on a single arbitrator has led in some cases to provision for arbitration by a board, usually of tripartite composition. Where this system is used, each party generally must name one member and the two persons so named select a third member to serve as a neutral chairman ; if they cannot agree on the third member the choice may be left to an outside authority such as the Minister of Labour or his delegate, or a judge or a private arbitration organisation. Under this system, it is expected that the person named by each party will be favourable to that side and that the chairman will be neutral and have the determining voice in reaching the final decision, which may be taken by a majority vote.

This tripartite approach has certain advantages in cases in which the issues are complex ones of principle requiring detailed examination. It is less necessary when the questions at issue are purely factual. It is argued that chairmanship of a tripartite board gives the arbitrator an opportunity to obtain greater clarification of complex issues. It also ensures that the issues are discussed on two occasions, first at the hearing and afterwards among the three members of the board. (The meeting of the board may be held either immediately after the close of the hearing or at a later date, when the members of the board, particularly the chairman, have had an opportunity to thoroughly examine the evidence. Sometimes in preparation for such a meeting the chairman will prepare a draft statement setting out the facts and contentions of the parties. Such sessions provide an opportunity to test the basis for the chairman's proposed award with the members appointed directly by the parties. Moreover, the chairman may on the same occasion have an opportunity to attempt to mediate the dispute, feeling out the parties' nominees as to their true opinions on the issues in dispute.) If unanimous, awards of tripartite boards tend to carry greater weight than awards by a single arbitrator. However, these benefits may be offset by delays occasioned in appointing the board, in arranging board meetings, in the frequent re-arguing of the case among the panel members after the hearing and in circulating a final written award for signature to the parties' nominees, who may append statements of concurrence or dissent with the majority decisions. The ultimate authority for decision still rests on a single person, the neutral chairman, and it would appear that little is gained in most cases by the establishment of such elaborate machinery.

PERMANENT OR AD HOC ARBITRATORS

If it has been decided that a single arbitrator shall be responsible for arbitrating grievances under the agreement, the parties may either decide on the appointment of a permanent arbitrator to arbitrate all disputes arising during the life of the agreement, or they may provide for an arbitrator to be chosen separately for each case that arises. In the first case, the name of the arbitrator is written into the parties' agreement as that of their regular arbitrator. The individual concerned may be employed full time, but more often works part-time, being on call when needed. One-time selection for the life of the agreement eliminates the time-consuming and often hostile discussions over who should arbitrate a specific dispute. It also does away with the risk of hastily selecting an arbitrator for a pending case without thorough examination of the person's background and ability and with the uncertainty associated with presenting a case to an unfamiliar arbitrator. Under this system, the parties have the advantage of dealing with an arbitrator whom they know, as well as continuity with past decisions. During their tenure such arbitrators develop familiarity with the undertaking as well as the details of its operations, and above all, a comprehensive and detailed understanding of the collective agreement from their repeated role in its interpretation and application. As a result there tends to be more rapid processing of cases and a lower cost, in the absence of the need to familiarise new arbitrators at successive hearings with the provisions of the agreement and the nature of the undertaking. Above all, with a permanent arbitrator, decisions tend to be more consistent with one another and provide the parties with a pattern of attitudes and precedents which will help them in dealing with similar disputes in the future.

Although in principle a permanent arbitrator is appointed for the duration of the collective agreement the parties may retain the right either jointly or singly to terminate the arbitrator's service at any time. The agreement may provide that the arbitrator remains "at the pleasure of both parties" and in this case if one of the parties is dissatisfied with the arbitrator, the appointment can be terminated.

A more common approach to the designation of the arbitrator is through separate selection for each case as it arises. Under this ad hoc selection system, the parties meet and mutually agree upon an arbitrator for each dispute. However, the agreement may empower the arbitrator chosen to hear a number of cases at one time if there are a number of grievances pending. Use of ad hoc arbitrators permits easy change of arbitrators when the parties so wish, although an arbitrator deemed satisfactory to both can be used repeatedly, even on an ad hoc basis. Parties with few disputes may find the ad hoc arrangement more convenient. Ad hoc selection also enables the parties to agree upon an arbitrator with special qualifications for a particular dispute. If the parties use ad hoc arbitrators, their agreement should provide a procedure and time limit for selection. Often the parties are unable to achieve agreement on selection of a particular arbitrator, and they should provide for an alternative method of appointment in anticipation of such a deadlock. In that connection it is important to provide a third party or an outside agency to help in the selection.

SELECTION SYSTEMS

For grievance arbitration to operate successfully, it is necessary for the parties to agree on a way of selecting an arbitrator in cases in which they are unable to agree amongst themselves. This problem will generally arise only in the case of ad hoc arbitrators since the parties may be expected not to provide for a permanent arbitrator if they cannot agree on the person concerned. It may, however, arise under an agreement providing for a permanent arbitrator if the arbitrator chosen by the parties subsequently loses their confidence and is released from further service.

If the agreement provides for the selection of ad hoc arbitrators, the parties will usually first try to agree on an arbitrator to hear a particular grievance. For this purpose they may have recourse to the appropriate government or private agency to obtain a list of qualified arbitrators. If the parties are unable to agree on the selection, different procedures may be followed. They should be specified in the collective agreement either in detail or by a provision to the effect that in the absence of agreement the rules for selecting an arbitrator laid down by a named designation agency (the competent government agency or private organisation) will be applicable. [1] This may be done, for example, by providing as follows :

---

[1] An example of the labour arbitration rules of a designating agency, the American Arbitration Association, is given in Appendix 3.

■ If the parties are unable to agree upon an arbitrator in   days after appeal to arbitration, either party may request [the designating agency] to submit a list of arbitrators from whom an arbitrator shall be designated in accordance with its rules and procedures.

One method is for the list to include an odd number of arbitrators (usually five) ; each side alternatively crosses out one name until only one name remains, which is the one chosen. Another is to send each of the parties an identical list of, for example, ten names. Each side strikes out the names of unacceptable arbitrators, lists the acceptable arbitrators in the order of their preference and returns the list to the designating agency. The person with the highest combined score is then designated by the agency as the arbitrator. If all the names are struck out by either or both of the parties, or if there is no mutually acceptable name remaining on the list, the designating agency may be asked to supply additional lists. If no agreement is then obtained, the agency is authorised to directly appoint an arbitrator previously unlisted.

On the other hand the parties may agree to request the designating agency to appoint the arbitrator directly instead of supplying a list. If the parties are unable to agree on naming an arbitrator and there is no designating agency, they may request a specified individual, such as the head of the government conciliation service or of the department of labour, or a judge or other mutually respected person, to appoint an arbitrator for them.

OTHER MATTERS

There are other matters which need to be specifically and clearly provided for in the arbitration agreement, such as the effect to be given to the award, the payment of the arbitrator's remuneration and other costs and the rules of procedure.

As regards the effect to be given to an award, national legislation may provide that arbitration awards shall in all cases be legally binding or that they shall be binding unless the parties provide otherwise. Whatever the legislative position, by agreeing to arbitration the parties generally give expression to a desire for final settlement of grievance disputes. The arbitration agreement may make this intention explicit by providing that "the award of the arbitrator shall be final and binding on the parties". Such a provision obligates the parties to abide by and implement the award, without its being possible for either of them to appeal to a higher authority (except in cases in which judicial action is permissible over the question of arbitrability or if the arbitrator exceeds his authority). It may happen, however, that one or both of the parties may not be willing or may not be persuaded to accept grievance arbitration except on condition that the arbitrator be empowered to make only advisory awards. Provisions to this effect may have to be accepted in the early stages of promoting grievance arbitration. Satisfactory experience may lead to later acceptance of the binding effect of the awards.

In addition, the agreement should state how the arbitrator's remuneration (unless the arbitrator agrees to serve free of charge) and other costs shall be divided between the parties. The usual practice is for the arbitrator's remuneration and any other common costs to be shared equally by the parties. In a very few cases the parties may allow the arbitrator to assess the liability for costs or may decide that the losing party shall meet most, if not all, of the costs. The fact that the parties have to defray these expenses is a strong reason for a final and binding award. In effect the parties are paying for an immediate and peaceful resolution of their dispute and for the maintenance of good relations between them.

As regards rules of procedure, the arbitrator is generally given considerable leeway in conducting the hearing. It is, however, essential to stipulate the time limit for issue of the award. [1] The parties should decide what other procedural requirements they want to lay down in the agreement. If the arbitrator is to be appointed with the help of a designating agency, the parties can provide that arbitration is subject to its rules of procedure and the relevant provisions of the agreement.

---

[1] See p. 59.

THE PARTIES' PREPARATION
OF A CASE

4

On the road to arbitration, the parties must take a number of steps. For each party, a successful outcome to the arbitration proceedings depends in substantial measure upon careful decisions on a number of pre-arbitration questions and upon adequate preparations.

DECISION TO GO TO ARBITRATION

The first question is, of course, whether the grievance should be brought to arbitration : should each side persist in its stand so far in the dispute ? Three tests must be met to make this determination : Is the case arbitrable under the terms of the parties' agreement ? Is it desirable to bring the case to arbitration ? Have procedural requirements been followed ?

If the arbitrability of an issue is challenged, the question of arbitrability will generally be decided by the arbitrator. But it is obviously a meaningless and expensive gesture to bring a matter to arbitration if the issue in dispute is beyond the scope of the arbitration agreement. Even if arbitration is provided free of charge to the parties, excessive processing of grievances that lie outside the jurisdiction of the arbitrator would needlessly tax the time and energy of the parties and the arbitrator and would tend to lessen the faith of the parties and the community in arbitration as an institution.

The second question, whether bringing the case to arbitration is desirable, is not as simple as it may appear. It would seem natural that each party should request arbitration only for cases in relation to which it feels that it has a good chance of winning ; it would be wasteful of time, money and energy to do otherwise. Moreover, continued lodging of frivolous or unjustified grievances may also tend to undermine the credibility of the moving party. Nonetheless cases often arise in which the outcome is uncertain but the issue at stake is important. Many cases arise from the parties' desire to settle a matter on which they have doubts. Often a particularly complex problem arises, with implications which go far beyond the obvious issue raised by the particular grievance. In such cases the arbitrator often performs a function that goes beyond merely deciding a particular issue : in interpreting the parties' agreement the arbitrator may provide them with guidance for their future relationship or point out weaknesses in language that may later result in changes in the agreement. In some cases the parties may not even wait for a specific grievance to arise but may call upon the arbitrator for an interpretation in a hypothetical situation of provisions that have created problems between them. The parties may also bring to arbitration some cases which they do not expect to win but which must be arbitrated for reasons of solidarity. Such cases may include a protest over an unjust disciplinary sanction imposed by a foreman whom his superiors are loath to disown for fear that it will reduce the foreman's future authority. Another type of case may result from strong pressures by workers on the union to put a case, though its officers may feel that adequate grounds are lacking. Such cases are sometimes sent to arbitration merely to maintain goodwill within the union and to show the members that the union will not shirk its responsibility of representing their interests.

There is another set of criteria that should be examined in determining whether a case should be referred to arbitration. Have the preliminary procedural requirements for arbitration been met ? Most arbitration agreements specify the time limits and form of appeals. Cases are often thrown out by the arbitrator because of the complainant's failure to comply with various requirements of the appeal procedure. Sometimes an appeal is not made in writing as required by the agreement, is made too late, or is made without having first exhausted the prior steps in the grievance procedure specified in the agreement. It is obviously pointless to undertake the preparation and presentation of a case when it suffers from such procedural defects. If too late to invoke arbitration, it is far better to wait until a similar issue is raised in the future, and then be sure to take all necessary steps to send the later case to arbitration. Needless to say, when a substantial procedural defect is uncovered that will bar arbitration, the party concerned would be well advised to correct its own methods of operation as a safeguard against the recurrence of such oversights in the future.

DEFINITION OF THE ISSUE

Once it is decided to submit a case to arbitration, it would be to the mutual advantage of the parties to get together and seek agreement on the issue to be arbitrated. In some cases, jointly submitted to arbitration, the issue will ordinarily be agreed upon by the parties in advance. Otherwise a statement of the issue will be attempted by the arbitrator at the outset of the hearing. In any event it is essential to define the issue to be resolved at the earliest possible stage, so that the parties are at least in agreement over what they disagree about. This agreement, or understanding, is vital to each party's preparations for the case, so that its full energies may be devoted to the core of the dispute, and not dissipated on peripheral or irrelevant issues. Sometimes efforts to seek such agreement bring home to the parties that they are really not in dispute at all or that they were arguing over a trivial matter. If the parties are able to agree as early as possible on the issue to be submitted to arbitration, the system will function more quickly and efficiently.

ASCERTAINMENT OF THE FACTS

Preparing for the arbitration hearing involves mastery of the facts involved in the particular dispute as well as of the relevant provisions of the collective agreement and of the past practice of the parties in relation to matters relevant to the dispute. It also requires the marshalling of all other evidence that will help convince the arbitrator of the merits of the party's position or at the very least ensure that the arbitrator has all the background information needed to understand the issues involved and come to an intelligent decision.

Elucidation of the factual background of the dispute is essential, particularly if the dispute involves discipline. Sometimes, if only one issue is involved, the parties may agree upon the facts and present the arbitrator with an agreed statement of what took place ; but in most cases it is up to each party to present its version of the facts to the arbitrator and to prepare for possible contradiction or challenge of its statement by the opposite side. Thus investigation of the facts and circumstances of the dispute is of great importance. The investigation should aim at ascertaining who and what are involved in the dispute.

The grievant's name and address should be ascertained, as well as particulars such as the following, to the extent relevant to the dispute : classification, duties, rate of pay, seniority, past positions, disciplinary record, attitude and job performance.

It is of immediate importance to ascertain that a written grievance adequately states the issue, so that a proper case is put up on the right issue. If the grievance as lodged is vague, it is essential to find out what exactly are the complaints. Once the grievance is clearly formulated, the next step is to ascertain exactly what transpired to lead to the lodging of the grievance.

Who were the individuals involved in the occurrence ? What do they know about the circumstances surrounding the grievance ? In disciplinary cases this may entail interviewing all possible witnesses who have knowledge of the event, regardless of which side they may testify for, and a careful reconstruction of every move leading up to the disciplinary action. Even in non-disciplinary cases it is important to build up a bank of factual information to buttress the case. This may require interviewing witnesses who are outside the establishment, such as doctors, police officers and neighbours of the grievant, who might provide evidence to support the party's case. Expert witnesses can be called to testify, but such witnesses may prove to be expensive. If the issue involves the meaning of the agreement or the nature of past practice, it will be necessary to ascertain what actually occurred in a negotiation (including what was and was not accepted) or in a prior grievance meeting, and this may also require interviewing witnesses to such negotiation or meeting. Since individuals may be forgetful or may colour their testimony for various personal motives, as many witnesses as possible should be interviewed.

COLLECTION OF RELEVANT RECORDS

Apart from calling witnesses and providing oral evidence the strongest means of buttressing the party's position is to submit written records. The relevant records will, of course, vary from case to case, but there are certain basic documents that are essential for all cases. They may be in the possession of the other side, but both parties will be expected to co-operate in making either the originals or copies of the necessary documents available. The documents in question include personal records of the participants, the current agreement, and perhaps even past agreements if there is a question of changed language or interpretation. The written statement of grievance, together with any annotations regarding its treatment at various stages of the grievance procedure, is essential. In a disciplinary case copies of the prior disciplinary forms are important, as well as information concerning the way in which earlier similar cases were dealt with. Often the company rules, various memoranda of understanding and correspondence between the parties will be relevant, as may be prior awards of arbitrators on related issues between these same two parties. Sometimes it may be necessary to go outside the undertaking for relevant exhibits, such as medical, hospital or police records, copies of medical prescriptions, and perhaps even municipal ordinances, statutes, and court decisions that may have a bearing on the case. Arbitration decisions by other arbitrators in similar cases involving other undertakings and unions are often of interest to the arbitrator in that they may suggest a line of reasoning. When an important witness is unable to attend, sworn affidavits are sometimes used. They are, of course, subject to challenge because the other party cannot cross-examine the witness, and the parties may therefore agree to take depositions jointly when witnesses have to be interviewed away from the hearing. However, affidavits are generally accepted without question.

It is often helpful to the arbitrator to have pictorial evidence. For this reason photographs, charts, plans of the plant facilities and maps may be valuable, particularly if the hearing is held in a place away from the plant itself. Representatives appointed to prepare a case may find it desirable to visit the site of the undertaking where the dispute arose to gain greater familiarity with places referred to during the presentation of the case.

PREPARATION OF ARGUMENTS

Once all the relevant facts and supporting material have been collected, it becomes easier for a party to prepare the arguments it will submit to the arbitrator. In the light of the agreement between the parties, each of them will attempt to show that the facts must lead to a particular finding in its favour. The arguments must be prepared with care, and must find support in the parties' agreement, understanding and past practice. It is common for the parties to rely on specific provisions to support their contentions, and in some cases multiple arguments may be presented. The greatest emphasis should naturally be placed upon key or pivotal arguments.

The agreement must be carefully examined to discover the provisions that support the party's position and those that might be cited by the other side. Any relevant legislation and judicial decisions should also be examined, as well as any other relevant documents, rules, correspondence and evidence of past practice. The remedy provided for similar or related grievances should also be looked into in order to buttress the party's case. Arguments of common humanity or common sense may be put forward to excuse or justify condonation of certain conduct, to indicate the reasonableness of management or labour action, or to seek mitigation of the penalty imposed. These arguments may be particularly important in cases in which the terms of the agreement are ambiguous or in which the written agreement is at variance with the practice followed.

To stress consistency, it is important to refer to prior arbitration awards involving the same parties. It is somewhat less important, and certainly not imperative to refer to arbitration awards concerning disputes between other parties, but it may be useful to learn how other parties have approached similar issues and how arbitrators have reacted to their arguments.

Arguments must be prepared anticipating the position, evidence and interpretations of the other side. This is essential if the opponents' case is to be effectively rebutted. It is likewise important for each side to tie its arguments to the factual material introduced at the outset of the hearing.

It is important to argue the merits of the case separately from the remedies. For example, the management of a firm may contend that its action was appropriate and should be sustained ; but it will often find it worthwhile to argue alternatively that if the arbitrator finds that the management did act improperly, the appropriate remedy should be less than that advocated by the union. By the same token, a trade union which argues that a worker was unjustly subject to a disciplinary sanction may find it advisable to request a reduction in the penalty (for example substitution of a fine or suspension for dismissal) if it should be found that there was some justification for disciplinary action by the employer.

SELECTION OF SPOKESMEN

Once the arguments have been worked out the individual best suited to put the party's case should be selected. Usually one official from the management side and one from the union will be selected by their principals to put their respective cases. Frequently the parties will call upon the individuals who served as their spokesmen at the earlier stages of the grievance procedure. Ordinarily management and union representatives are sufficiently familiar with the facts involved in a case and can be expected to learn to put a case and interpret a contract as clearly and often as effectively as trained lawyers. However, the parties may hire professional counsel when complex legal issues are involved. Lawyers who understand collective bargaining and grievance handling can be very useful, but hiring legal counsel often raises the cost of arbitration beyond what many employers and unions can afford. If lawyers are hired the hearing may have to be delayed until they are available to plead. If they are employed, moreover, it is necessary to guard against giving an atmosphere of formal litigation to the arbitration proceedings.

TESTING THE STRENGTH OF A CASE

Each party should prepare an outline or brief of its case for study and use at the hearing. As indicated earlier, the selection of the most suitable witnesses is of prime importance. When a number of interviewed individuals have contributed to the reconstruction of events it is unnecessary, and in fact damaging, to have more than one or two give evidence on what took place. The persons selected should be the ones who know the most at first hand and who have a reliable memory for past details. Sometimes the best witnesses are not readily available and the party must make special arrangements to have them attend the hearing. This may involve paying expenses or reimbursing lost earnings for those involved. It is essential that all witnesses should have an over-all view of the party's case as well as of the relationship of their testimony to that case. Perhaps the best way to test the strength of a party's case is to actually go through a mock hearing sequence. One advantage of such a procedure is that it involves considering the opponent's case as well, and having individuals serve as witnesses for the other side. This not only provides a test for the party's witnesses, particularly under cross-examination, but more importantly subjects the party's entire case to careful scrutiny under the stress of simulated opposition. After such a mock session, the weaknesses of a case are more apparent, and the party concerned has an opportunity to discover further evidence or arguments for presentation at the real arbitration hearing. If a party is not convinced of the strength of its case at this point it would be wise either to withdraw altogether or to seek an offer of compromise or settlement from the other side. This would avoid both the cost of arbitration and the risk of losing the case.

SELECTION OF THE ARBITRATOR

When a definite decision is taken to proceed to arbitration, the arbitrator will be selected according to the procedure provided for in the arbitration agreement (except, of course, in the case of a permanent arbitrator). Certain cases may require a particular technical expertise which the average arbitrator may lack. The parties may specify these requirements in the provision of the agreement dealing with the selection of arbitrators. More likely, they will both recognise the need for expertise when selecting an arbitrator for a particular case. This is particularly true for cases involving incentive wage rates, complex interpretation of the agreement, insurance coverage questions and the like. Sometimes arbitrators with the requisite expertise are not readily available or not agreeable to both parties. In such cases the parties must try to ensure that the arbitrator acquires the necessary knowledge and understanding before the case is heard.

If the parties have requested the assistance of a designating agency the list of possible arbitrators sent to them would be accompanied by accounts of their background and experience ; but the parties usually go beyond such accounts in order to satisfy themselves as to an arbitrator's impartiality and acceptability. There are several ways by which a party can ascertain, or at least gain some insight into, an arbitrator's position on various issues. If the arbitrator has acted as such in previous cases, the most direct way is to examine the resulting awards, where available. It may be possible to obtain the texts from the parties in those cases or from the designating agency, which should maintain a compilation of awards in cases in which it has been involved. Less effective but of prime interest to the parties is examination of the arbitrators' past experience, particularly in the industrial relations field. Such information may be obtained, for example, from past articles, speeches and pronouncements if the arbitrator has engaged or participated in discussions of labour-management problems. Any individual who is committed to one side on a particular issue will undoubtedly be unacceptable to the other side. In brief, the value of the investigation just described is to assure the party concerned that the arbitrator may not have possibly prejudged the issue and that the dispute will receive a fair and impartial hearing.

ARRANGEMENT AND CONDUCT OF THE HEARING

5

Once the arbitrator has been chosen and the parties are ready to proceed with their presentation, arrangements have to be made for the hearing itself. The person selected as arbitrator should be informed of the selection and ascertained to be available.

PLACE AND TIME

Usually the parties are able to agree upon a place for the hearing. Government-provided facilities may be available for holding arbitration hearings in some countries. Company offices or conference rooms may be used, this being particularly convenient if there is any prospect that the arbitrator will visit the work site or examine the operation to which the dispute relates. If there is opposition to holding the hearing on company premises, a local hotel conference room might be more acceptable. The use of such facilities entails additional expense, which might be shared by the two parties. If the workplace or company office is far removed from a built-up area or inaccessible to the arbitrator, the parties may agree in some cases to hold the hearing in some other mutually convenient place or in the arbitrator's office. This approach is convenient only if there is no need to visit the workplace itself, if the number of witnesses is small, and if the cost of moving the hearing is relatively low for all concerned. Generally the parties will decide on the location of the hearing. When there is a choice of locations the arbitrator may have a preference and may so inform the parties, who will naturally try to meet the arbitrator's wishes in that respect.

The proceedings should be open to all interested parties, in addition to the people who will give evidence or advise the spokesmen for either side. However, an attempt should be made to ensure that not too many people attend : large audiences tend to lead to more formal proceedings and stimulate the spokesmen for both sides into rallying the public to their cause rather than presenting the case to the arbitrator. In any event the room in which the hearing is held should be big enough to hold all the people planning to attend. There should be space for the parties to sit and write, and enough chairs for all participants. In most instances the hearing is held at a single table with the arbitrator at one end and one of the parties on each of the two sides of the table. A separate place might be set aside for witnesses to give evidence, although frequently they speak from wherever they may be seated around the table.

The hearing room should be light, airy, and quiet. Efforts should be made to restrict interruptions by telephone or outsiders. This is particularly important when hearings are held in company offices. Extraneous noises can seriously hinder the parties and the arbitrator from concentrating on the case.

Arranging for the time of the hearing is often more complicated than arranging for the location, since times have to be found to suit not only the arbitrator but also the spokesmen (possibly practising lawyers) for management and the union, as well as the work schedule of others whose attendance is required. In most cases, however, the parties should be able to set the time for the hearing with minimal difficulty, usually offering a series of available dates to all of the participants, and readily coming to a mutually acceptable choice. If the issue in dispute is a pressing one, such as a discharge or dismissal, the parties generally expedite the procedure to have the hearing squeezed into otherwise busy times.

TRANSCRIPTS

In the course of their discussions on the time and place of the hearing, the parties may be able to agree on other aspects of the hearing. Transcripts are usually not required by arbitrators, who will generally take copious notes. There are some cases, however, in which a transcript may be important and desired by the arbitrator, such as a case involving contradictory evidence, or one in which the issue involves complicated and technical references. Where credibility is in dispute, the arbitrator may prefer to be free to observe the demeanour of the witnesses, and to rely on a transcript to record the content of the evidence put forward. However, transcripts tend to be quite costly and frequently contribute little to the efficiency of the hearing. The formality which they engender tends to restrict the comments of the parties who recognise that their every word is being recorded for posterity : a transcript might even militate against informal efforts at settlement of the dispute during the arbitration proceedings. Where transcripts are prepared, they should be available to all concerned. Arbitrators should refuse to receive a transcript that is not made available for distribution to both of the parties to the hearing. The cost of the transcript may be shared by the parties.

Agreement might also be reached before the hearing on certain other matters such as release time for union witnesses and the responsibility for bringing a sufficient number of copies of pertinent documents to the hearing for distribution to those concerned.

OPENING OF THE HEARING

Generally all of the parties will convene in the designated room at the time agreed upon for the start of the hearing. The parties will usually know each other, but the arbitrator and some of the witnesses may be new to one or both of the parties. Thus the initial step is the mutual introduction of the people present. The spokesmen for the parties should identify themselves. Partly because an arbitration hearing is generally a new experience for most of the people attending, particularly the witnesses, the proceedings should preferably be informal by comparison with ordinary court cases, unless hostility between the parties requires that a more formal procedure should be followed. In any event there is a certain sequence that is usually observed to ensure an orderly consideration of the case : the rules for the hearing are made known, and the factual evidence for each party is then submitted, with ample opportunity for cross-questioning of witnesses, after which the parties are given full opportunity to argue the merits of their respective cases.

An initial procedural question to be considered, if not already agreed upon by the parties when arranging for the hearing, is whether witnesses should testify under oath. Although this feature of formal legal proceedings is also often a feature of arbitration hearings, particularly in cases in which credibility is at stake, it seems better to avoid the formal swearing in of witnesses.

STATEMENT OF THE ISSUE

As suggested above,[1] it is most desirable that the parties should have reached agreement before the actual hearing with regard to the exact issue submitted to arbitration. Not only will this save time at the hearing but also it will help the parties to narrow the issues between them and to improve the preparation of their respective cases. If no such agreement has been reached before the hearing, the arbitrator often serves as a mediator in

---

[1] On p. 32.

helping the parties to reach agreement on the issue to be arbitrated. In disciplinary matters the framing of an issue is relatively simple. Usually it is phrased in the following language : "Did the Company violate the parties' agreement of [date] when it [suspended, discharged or otherwise disciplined] worker X ?"

Agreement upon the statement of issue in other matters is frequently more difficult to obtain. Usually each party has its own proposal regarding the statement of the issue, and there is often understandable reluctance to agree to the statement proposed by the opponent. On this point the arbitrator may succeed in helping the parties to agree by proposing other possible statements of the issue. If the parties do not agree on which specific provisions of the agreement are applicable, the arbitrator may solve the problem by including reference to the provisions cited by both parties or to both the cited provisions and "all other relevant provisions of the parties' agreement". If conflict over this issue threatens to take up too much of the total time available for the hearing, the arbitrator might suggest that the statement of the issue be phrased as follows : "What action shall be taken in relation to the grievance lodged by worker X on [date] ?" Unfortunately, however, the written grievance itself may have been poorly worded and may have an emphasis quite different from the real issue as it has developed between the parties in the course of their pre-arbitration discussions.

The formulation of the issue has a direct bearing on the remedy to be awarded if it is found that the agreement was violated. To avoid any possible doubt on whether the arbitrator is being requested to award a remedy, the statement of the issue should also include such a request. Usually the question whether the agreement has been violated is followed by "If so, to what remedy is the grievant entitled ?", or "If so, what shall the remedy be ?"

OPENING STATEMENT OF EACH PARTY'S CASE

Once the issue to be arbitrated is agreed upon, the arbitrator begins to hear the parties' presentation of their case. Up to this point the arbitrator has had no knowledge of the case other than perhaps the parties' statement of the issue and any written submissions that may have been made. By contrast the representatives of each side have been long immersed in the dispute and know its background more thoroughly. Accordingly, it is desirable that each side should first make a concise statement of what it intends to prove and argue during the presentation of the case. Such opening statements give the arbitrator an understanding of the objectives of the parties at the hearing and an over-all view which makes it easier to follow the presentation of the evidence. Sometimes such opening statements are offered in writing, but they are better made orally. No evidence is introduced at this stage, merely a general statement of what it is intended to prove.

Although arbitration proceedings are not as strict as court proceedings in matters of burden of proof, generally the moving party, that is, the side which brought the grievance (usually the worker or the union), will begin the presentation. In disciplinary cases, however, it is desirable that the first opening statement should be made by the employer's spokesman who should afterwards also plead first, on the theory that the employer took the disciplinary action and is likely to have specific knowledge of the facts involved. Such an approach greatly expedites and simplifies the procedure.

PRESENTATION OF EVIDENCE

Once the opening statements have been made it is time to proceed to the presentation of the evidence to prove the facts that will underpin the arguments of the parties concerning the alleged violation of their agreement. Occasionally [1] the parties will have met in advance and agreed to a statement of the facts, obviating any need for each side to call witnesses in support of its factual contentions. In such an agreed statement the parties jointly relate all pertinent facts and jointly submit them to the arbitrator. In some cases there is an agreed statement concerning only some of the facts, and then each side submits other factual evidence which it deems to be significant.

If there is no agreed statement of the facts, the party that made the first summary statement of its case generally proceeds with the submission of its evidence. This is done as in a court of law, but without the latter's formality. The persons who were most closely concerned with the issue in dispute are generally called upon to explain what happened. Their statements are frequently supported by "exhibits"—records, transcripts, files, photographs, and the like. Witnesses are examined first by the side calling them. The spokesman for that side continues to ask questions until the answers have provided a complete picture of what that side seeks to present to the arbitrator. No effort should be made to lead witnesses to the "right" answers ; the spokesman should instead put questions that enable the witnesses to testify from their own memory concerning what occurred. Each witness, after initial examination, is subject to questioning by the spokesman for the other side. Such cross-examination is intended either to clarify the facts or to call in question the credibility of the witnesses. It seeks to induce witnesses to add to their evidence statements that detract from their earlier statements or buttress the opponent's case. In cross-examination the representatives of the

---

[1] As stated on p. 33.

parties have greater freedom to lead witnesses to make a desired statement, but generally this questioning is confined to subjects raised by the witnesses in their answers in the direct examination. When cross-examination is concluded the party calling a witness may engage in further direct examination, either to correct misinterpretations from the witness's answers to cross-examination or perhaps to open new fields which had not been examined before. There is a right of cross-examination after this re-direct questioning as well. It is the arbitrator's duty to see to it that all relevant evidence is submitted and that decorum is maintained in the questioning without intimidation or abuse of witnesses by the opposing spokesman.

This procedure is followed to admit the evidence of each of the witnesses until the moving party has exhausted its roster of witnesses. Sometimes the list of witnesses used is an extensive one. Efforts should be made to limit the witnesses to those with the best knowledge of what happened, and to avoid needless repetition or support of their statements. When the roster of witnesses for one side is exhausted, it becomes the opponent's turn to introduce its evidence and exhibits through its witnesses. The same procedure is then followed with direct examination, cross-examination, and further direct examination and cross-examination until all the evidence has been produced and all of the witnesses of both parties have been given an opportunity to be heard, examined and cross-examined.

Sometimes new evidence is introduced to the surprise of the other party. If the arbitrator is convinced that the new evidence adds an unexpected and important new element to the case, the surprised party should on request be granted a postponement to study the implications of such evidence and to prepare an answer. Postponements are also often granted if an important witness is unavailable for the hearing.

The exhibits that are offered by the parties in support of their witnesses' testimony are kept by the arbitrator and marked as exhibits for the side presenting them, being usually numbered chronologically in order of presentation. Often there are exhibits that are jointly offered as being mutually supporting, such as the parties' agreement, memorandum of understanding, and the like ; these are also numbered in the order of their introduction into evidence. Copies should be provided for all parties.

In some cases the arbitrator might improve his grasp of the problem by a personal visit to the place where the dispute arose. Such action might be particularly important when the layout of facilities in the plant or the contents of an operation are involved. Such a visit might be suggested either by the arbitrator or by one of the parties. Generally representatives from each side accompany the arbitrator to give the necessary explanations and answer questions.

PRESENTATION OF ARGUMENTS

After the arbitrator has been informed of the facts of the case the parties should proceed to interpret that evidence in support of their position, and put forward their arguments. The order of presentation is the same for arguments as for the factual material. The moving party usually starts. In many cases the party first lists its arguments and then proceeds to make them, with frequent specific reference to the evidence previously submitted. Reference is also made to particular provisions of the agreement under consideration (or to other provisions relevant to the case), to past practice of the parties where relevant and perhaps to the established practice in the industry as well. Sometimes the parties will agree to waive the oral presentation of their arguments, and to lodge written briefs setting out their arguments after the hearing instead. At other times, the parties will argue their cases orally and then lodge written briefs in addition. In most cases, oral pleading is regarded by the parties as constituting an adequate presentation of their views and unless the issue is particularly complex, involving a substantial amount of citation of prior decisions and the like, the arbitrator will not request post-hearing briefs. This will avoid the delays that may occur if written briefs are to be submitted. If briefs are not lodged and no transcript is to be supplied the case is actually closed when the hearing is concluded. If briefs are to be lodged the parties agree on the date for their submission to the arbitrator, at which time the briefs are also exchanged between the parties. It is generally agreed when briefs are to be lodged that there shall be no rebuttal thereto, that the briefs shall not introduce new material or raise new issues, and that failure to lodge a brief by the time agreed upon shall constitute a waiver of the right to lodge a brief at all. The briefs generally outline the party's case and arguments and are valuable only to the extent that they may shorten the hearing itself or clarify extensive factual details or arguments for the arbitrator.

After the two sides have put their closing arguments or lodged their briefs, the submission of further statements, evidence and arguments should be prohibited, unless there is an agreement of the parties or a decision of the arbitrator to the contrary. The arbitrator will be expected to make the award within a reasonable time after the closing of the case. Under some agreements or rules there is a specific deadline, frequently thirty days, by which the award must be issued. In simple cases a shorter period may be sufficient, particularly if a written award is not required. The arbitrator has no further authority, power or responsibility once the award has been rendered. Any reopening of the proceedings thereafter must be undertaken at the joint request of the parties.

THE ARBITRATOR'S ROLE
AT THE HEARING

At the hearing the function of the arbitrator is to conduct the proceedings in such a manner that sufficient evidence and arguments will be produced to enable the case to be properly decided. The arbitrator is also responsible for deciding what evidence is to be admitted and must decide whether to accept evidence that is held to be inadmissible by one side or the other. In some cases the parties may not adequately meet their obligation of presenting the case fully, and the arbitrator may find it necessary to ask questions of the parties or their witnesses. Generally the arbitrator waits for the respective spokesmen to elicit crucial information from the witnesses. The witnesses may be asked additional questions by the arbitrator if the situation appears confused or if relevant information is not forthcoming. Questions by the arbitrator on the evidence are generally asked of witnesses at the conclusion of their testimony. Questions on the arguments are usually asked of the parties directly during or at the conclusion of their arguing the cases. Arbitrators are expected to play a more active role than judges in labour tribunals or ordinary courts, and may at times desire to conduct an independent investigation of some aspect of the case before them. This may involve personal visits to the plant site, as noted above, or discussions with experts who were not present at the hearing. In such a case it is important to have the acquiescence of the parties to such an investigation or to provide them with an opportunity to comment on the information obtained therefrom.

The arbitrator's being a quasi-judicial function, the award is expected to be based upon the evidence presented : it is therefore essential that the arbitrator should refrain from contact with either party outside the presence of the other, at any rate without its permission. This requirement often effectively precludes even ordinary social intercourse with one of the parties during the presentation of the case. Once the hearings are concluded the arbitrator has to be wary about contact with either of the parties until the award is rendered.

In some cases the arbitrator may feel that the issue in dispute between the parties is so narrow as to be readily amenable to settlement by the parties themselves without the need for an award. In such cases an arbitrator who knows the parties well, and feels it to be appropriate, may with their knowledge and approval attempt to mediate the dispute. The parties who institute arbitration proceedings may not want the arbitrator to mediate, but mediation may on occasion prove to be a more effective way of resolving disputes and may save the parties time and expense. There is little question that it is better for disputes to be settled by the parties themselves than by an outsider.

PROBLEMS OF PROOF

6

Arbitration has evolved with a minimum of the formalities that characterise judicial proceedings. This informality particularly affects questions of evidence : the strict rules followed by the courts regarding acceptability of evidence tend to be avoided in arbitration proceedings. In arbitration, unlike cases up for trial by jury, there is little need for protecting the finder of fact from extraneous or partially misleading information. The individual specifically designated by the parties to hear the case will be one whose judgement they respect and who will generally have enough sense and understanding of the matters at issue to recognise what information is relevant and what is extraneous to the decision that will have to be reached. Also, the arbitration of a grievance dispute is generally not compulsory but voluntary. The relationship between the parties is an ongoing one rather than a single confrontation and generally the parties will therefore have developed an informal approach to such matters. However, if the parties have followed a more formal approach arbitrators should adapt their methods of proceeding.

The procedure for arbitration hearings has on the whole followed a pattern which has come to be widely accepted. Practice regarding admissibility of evidence and question of proof tends to be less strict than that followed in court proceedings. However, there are certain limits which enable the arbitrator to maintain control of the proceedings, to confine the hearing to relevant matters and to protect the parties from excessive repetition of evidence. In this connection, the rules laid down by the designating agency or by the parties in their collective agreement may specify that the arbitrator shall be the judge of the relevance of the evidence offered and that conformity to legal rules of evidence shall not be required. Arbitrators will accordingly listen to any evidence, information or testimony which they deem to be pertinent to the case and which they believe will help them to understand and decide the problems before them.

HEARSAY

One question which frequently arises concerns hearsay, i.e. cases in which witnesses give evidence second-hand, concerning what they were told had happened. Courts of law generally restrict the introduction of such hearsay evidence but in arbitration, by and large, evidence is not excluded because it is hearsay. Arbitrators would, of course, prefer to hear evidence from the original source, but hearsay evidence can be admitted on the understanding that the arbitrator knows it is hearsay and will accord it no more than its proper weight. Generally, little weight is given to hearsay unless it is supported by stronger direct evidence, or if it is contradicted by evidence that has stood up to cross-examination. Mere assertions or allegations are not proof. Evidence on anything said or done by anyone concerned should be listened to, and the experience and good judgement of the arbitrator relied upon to separate the truth from the untruth.

CREDIBILITY

One of the greatest problems for the arbitrator hearing factual evidence is to determine the credibility of witnesses. In judging credibility the arbitrator observes the manner of the witness while testifying, particularly under questioning by the opposite party, to discover the witness's character, emotional capacity, consistency and attitudes toward others at the hearing. The arbitrator would seek information on a witness's reputation, degree of experience, opportunity to observe the incident in question, interest and motivation, and above all on the probability that the witness will give true evidence in the circumstances.

FAILURE OF GRIEVANT TO TESTIFY

In courts of law in some countries the right of protection against self-incrimination is often invoked to justify the failure of a defendant to testify in a criminal case. While arbitrators would respect this refusal by the grievant in, for example, a case of theft, for which criminal proceedings might be pending, the failure of a grievant to testify on a point without criminal implications is likely to raise a question in the mind of the arbitrator. The grievant may refrain from testifying for fear of appearing to be a confused or inadequate witness, but the arbitrator may feel that the failure to testify leaves a crucial gap in the case and may become sceptical of the merits of the grievant's claim.

IRRELEVANCE AND IMMATERIALITY

In courts of law a good deal of important evidence may be excluded when objected to as being irrelevant and immaterial. Arbitrators are not bound by this rule, but can discourage the introduction of evidence which they feel will be of no help in deciding the issue. It is, however, important to remember the cathartic value of arbitration, during which the parties and the witnesses can unburden themselves about what to them is most important evidence and material. Part of the arbitrators' function is to listen to such evidence although they may not attach any great significance to it, so as to let the parties feel that they have had an opportunity to fully present their case. An arbitrator can always sort out the relevant evidence from the irrelevant afterwards. Much of the evidence that may be introduced at the early stages of arbitration proceedings may not appear to be germane to the development of a party's case until later in the proceedings, but to exclude evidence which at first appears irrelevant might be substantially detrimental to the presentation of that case.

IMPROPERLY OBTAINED EVIDENCE

Arbitrators are frequently confronted with questions concerning improperly obtained evidence. They should be reluctant to consider evidence forcibly taken from an employee's locked locker, even though on company property, and should look askance at a forcibly extracted confession.

STATEMENTS MADE AT EARLIER STAGES
IN THE GRIEVANCE PROCEDURE

Admission of evidence concerning statements made at earlier stages in the discussion of a grievance may cause some difficulty for arbitrators who are vitally concerned with the preservation of the grievance procedure and do not want to sap its foundations. It is generally considered that an arbitrator may allow reference to statements made by the grievant at earlier stages of the grievance procedure, as well as statements made at those stages by other persons in the grievant's presence without contradiction by the grievant. References to other statements made in the course of the initial grievance proceedings are generally excluded.

Parties sometimes keep written minutes of the initial grievance proceedings and frequently attempt to introduce such material during the arbitration hearing. The arbitrator will on occasion consider such minutes if they are drawn up jointly, or drawn up by one side and then distributed and commented on by both. He will undoubtedly exclude minutes that have been drawn up by one side only, if the other side objects to their admission as evidence.

Another troublesome question is that of offers of compromise. In this respect there is a general belief, carried over from the ordinary courts, that proposals for settlement of a particular grievance have little relationship to proof of innocence or guilt, since the arbitrator may not know the whole nature of the proposed settlement, i.e. exactly why a settlement might have been made or in exchange for what other benefits. Arbitrators are loath to accept inferences drawn from alleged offers to compromise for fear that if they do so they may deter the parties from making such offers in future disputes.

EVIDENCE OF INTENTIONS
WHEN CONCLUDING THE AGREEMENT

Although the arbitrator lacks the authority to change the terms of the parties' agreement, such agreements are often drafted in ambiguous language which gives rise to differing interpretations. In such situations the arbitrator may be offered evidence of what the parties intended when they drafted the agreement. Thus a practice that had prevailed for many years before the agreement was adopted may lead to the interpretation that the contested wording was intended to endorse past practice. Conversely, the evidence may show that the terms of the agreement were specifically intended to counter prior practice. In either case, the conduct of the parties during the negotiation of the terms in question will be relevant to determining the intended meaning of the provisions in their agreement.

CIRCUMSTANCIAL EVIDENCE

In many cases arbitrators as well as judges are not offered solely direct evidence, i.e. evidence of witnesses to a particular event : quite frequently circumstantial evidence is offered with the intent of convincing the arbitrator that a certain event did take place although not directly witnessed. For example, evidence that material produced at the plant was found in the worker's possession outside the plant would be circumstantial evidence concerning an alleged theft : such evidence would raise the inference of theft, although there may have been no witness to the actual removal of the item from the plant. Generally the arbitrator will admit such evidence as being of probative value, although the weight given to it will probably be less than that given to direct evidence.

SUBPOENA POWER

Often certain evidence which one party feels to be essential to its case is not in its possession and the party is unable to obtain it. In an ordinary court of law, the judge would possess subpoena power by which the possessor of the evidence could be ordered to submit it to the court. Arbitrators may feel an equal need for such evidence, but unless there is legislation granting them the right to subpoena, they lack such power. In practice, however, the lack of subpoena power does not create much of a problem in efforts to obtain evidence. If the arbitrator wants certain evidence it can be asked for, even if on behalf of the party which seeks it to bolster its case. The party requested to provide such evidence will usually do so out of fear of prejudicing its case before the arbitrator, who will naturally give some weight to the failure of the party to produce requested information or documentation. The weight given to such refusal is dependent upon its confidentiality and its relevance to the case at hand. A party to arbitration proceedings usually has little difficulty in obtaining prior to the hearing all the evidence it may wish from the other party, having regard to the effect which later conflict with the arbitrator may have on the case.

NEW EVIDENCE

Often the arbitrator is confronted with an objection raised by a party to new evidence that was already available earlier but had not been submitted at earlier stages of the grievance procedure. Although the arbitrator will be anxious to have all relevant information supplied in order to allow a complete review of the evidence before making the award, the failure of one of the parties to present certain evidence at earlier stages of the grievance procedure raises suspicions with regard to its relevance, to the good faith of the party belatedly offering the evidence, and to the repercussions the late admission of the evidence might have on the processing of grievances in the future. Generally such evidence is admitted if relevant. If the arbitrator believes the new evidence to be sufficiently important the parties may be urged to resume their direct negotiations on the grievance, in hope of a settlement. At any rate the arbitrator will offer to adjourn the hearing until the other party has had time to examine the new evidence and prepare a response.

A somewhat different situation arises if new evidence is discovered when the dispute is already before the arbitrator. If the evidence is discovered at that stage, its admission usually raises no questions of bad faith. The arbitrator will probably admit the evidence, if decisive, giving the opposing side sufficient time to prepare a reply, even if that requires adjournment of the hearing until the reply is prepared.

New evidence may also be discovered after the close of the hearing. When this occurs the arbitrator will receive such evidence only if submitted by both parties or if it is agreed in advance that the other party will have an opportunity for later cross-questioning. When such evidence is deemed sufficiently important for the parties to bring it to the attention of the arbitrator, the latter will endeavour to reopen the hearing with the consent of the parties to permit examination and cross-examination.

THE ARBITRATION AWARD

7

An arbitration award, or decision on the settlement of the dispute, may take many forms, but the most careful attention must be paid by the arbitrator to its preparation.

The arbitrator's award may be rendered orally or in writing. The option chosen will depend on the needs and wishes of the parties concerned and on the nature of the case. In some cases, if the issues are straightforward and consist mainly of questions of fact and if it is desired to limit costs as far as possible, an oral award may suffice. An oral award may likewise be desirable in some cases in which circumstances require an immediate decision. It is particularly valuable in dismissal cases or if action by the parties is suspended pending the arbitrator's ruling and where other commitments preclude the arbitrator's immediate preparation of a written award. Such oral decisions may be subsequently reduced to writing and submitted to the parties. In any event, it is for the parties to decide on the method followed.

The issuing of an oral award immediately at the conclusion of the hearing should be avoided because it does not afford the arbitrator sufficient time to carefully weigh the evidence or adequately reflect before making a decision. It is also desirable to avoid the impression of hasty judgement or the impression that so weak a case was made by the losing party that deliberation on the part of the arbitrator was unnecessary. Such an impression could well lead to resentment that might make the award difficult to enforce. It might also be detrimental to the arbitrator's continuing acceptability.

ASSESSMENT OF THE EVIDENCE

In preparing awards arbitrators examine the evidence offered by the parties, as well as their arguments, in the light of the parties' agreement, past practice and the like ; they function alone, relying on their notes, any transcript or briefs supplied and any exhibits submitted during the hearing ; they consult no one for advice or further information unless specifically authorised to do so by the parties. Careful note-taking has its rewards, for certain evidence, not apparently vital at the time when it was given, may become a key to the arbitrator's decision : the record of a hearing, either in the form of a verbatim transcript or of notes taken by the arbitrator at the time, will have new meaning in the light of the parties' argumentation. This is particularly true in cases involving disputed sequences of events or varying statements made by several witnesses, as in a disciplinary case.

The arbitrator must often weigh conflicting testimony, determine the weight to be attached to hearsay or gossip and the relevance of circumstantial evidence, and determine whether the party responsible for convincing the arbitrator has done so. In the case of conflicting testimony the arbitrator must decide who is telling the truth. Evidence given by a witness having a stake in the outcome of the proceedings will be subject to greater scrutiny, although the witness should not be disqualified *a priori*. The failure of an important witness to give evidence at a hearing is bound to have some effect on the arbitrator's deliberations. This is particularly true in disciplinary cases in which the accuser is not present and the grievant is denied the right of cross-examination.

The arbitrator must also consider the evidence in the light of the parties' past relations and personal attitudes, and of the need for preservation and improvement of those relations in the future. In disciplinary and dismissal cases the arbitrator must be concerned with what has been the parties' practice in enforcing discipline for similar acts in the past, the relevance and weight of the grievant's past record, and whether the grievant's attitude is such as to make it possible to expect an improvement in his or her conduct.

INTERPRETATION OF THE AGREEMENT

The role of the arbitrator often includes responsibility for resolving ambiguities in the parties' agreement. Ambiguities exist when conflicting interpretations arise from the same text. A clear text is generally applied literally but often an apparently clear text is susceptible to differing interpretations. Moreover, the parties sometimes deliberately make a provision ambiguous to deal with differences that have not been truly resolved. The arbitrator must endeavour to discover what the parties intended and then make his award accordingly.

To reach a decision the entire agreement must be examined, as well as the provisions specifically cited, in the light of related provisions of the agreement. Supplementary agreements, certificates, letters, prior awards and other documents are also relevant in shaping the arbitrator's opinion. The cited provisions of the parties' agreement must be studied in their context, in the light of the parties' intent at the time of negotiations. Evidence of other proposed but rejected wording, the wording in similar sections of prior agreements, and practice that appears to be at variance with a particular provision, may all be relevant to determining the intent of the parties. Evidence concerning the course of the parties' negotiations often helps to resolve ambiguities. Such evidence may be oral, or may consist of minutes of the negotiating sessions or of documents setting out the parties' demands. Unsuccessful efforts to include certain provisions in an agreement will almost uniformly preclude the arbitrator from reading such provisions into the agreement. The arbitrator must determine the weight to be attached to general provisions when in seeming conflict with the specific terms of other provisions. Sometimes the arbitrator will as a matter of principle interpret the provision in such a way as to ensure that it will be in accord with other provisions of the agreement. The arbitrator is expected to give a reasonable interpretation of the agreement, but not to alter it; alterations must be left to the parties to arrange through negotiation between themselves.

Certain legal concepts used to help resolve ambiguities in statute law are equally applicable to the interpretation of collective agreements. Thus the concept of *inclusio unius est exclusio alterius* is generally followed to exclude unmentioned items from coverage when a series in a class are spelled out in the agreement. Likewise, the doctrine of *eiusdem generis,* giving coverage to other items of the same class when general words of inclusion follow a specific enumeration, is generally held to exclude from coverage items not in the same class. Specific language is usually held to prevail over general language.

PAST PRACTICE OF THE PARTIES

The practice of the parties may be considered to be as much a part of the parties' relationship as the provisions of the agreement. Indeed it can be held that past practice can be carried forward as one of the terms of employment and can become in a sense a part of the agreement. The practice of the parties is the most concrete manifestation of the relationship between them as they live under and apply their interpretations of the agreement. Thus evidence of past practice that has not been circumscribed or limited by subsequent agreements will have great bearing in determining the intent of the parties : arbitrators therefore recognise past practice as an essential component of the parties' relationship and place weight upon it in attempting to ascertain the true intent of the parties to the agreement or the manner in which the parties have adapted the agreement to the realities of the workshop. In some cases a consistent practice of the parties in contradiction to the written agreement will be viewed by the arbitrator as a reshaping or amending of the contract by mutual consent, an ongoing and consistent practice of the parties in direct violation of the written word in the contract being regarded in effect as a rewriting of the contract by the parties themselves. The weighing of the importance to be given to such practice in relation to the terms of the agreement may be crucial to the arbitrator's decision.

RELEVANCE OF OTHER AWARDS

Although prior arbitration awards may assist the arbitrator in understanding the issues and arriving at a fair and equitable settlement of the case, arbitrators should not place too much weight upon such awards since an attempt to follow precedent may create a strictly legalistic approach, similar to that followed in the ordinary courts, which the very concept of arbitration is intended to avoid. At the same time, however, arbitrators may wish to encourage publication of awards because of their educational value to the parties in learning how an arbitrator reasons in administering an agreement, in preparing for arbitration, and also in negotiations. Such published awards may help employers and trade unions to draft their agreements in terms that avoid the pitfalls found in other agreements. While relying on the parties to supply any precedents between them in prior awards, the arbitrator may also carry out research among published awards to learn of other arbitrators' rulings in comparable cases. Awards of other arbitrators in relation to grievances involving the same parties should be given considerable weight. If involving different parties, they may be cited for their reasoning or persuasiveness rather than for the decision reached.

RELEVANCE OF LEGISLATION
AND COURT DECISIONS

Despite the fact that an arbitration agreement creates a private substitute for litigation in the courts, arbitrators are generally influenced by relevant decisions of courts and other tribunals : they endeavour to work within the confines of the law, which provides the ultimate basis of their authority, and they avoid decisions that would be contrary to statutory provisions and judicial decisions interpreting those provisions. They must therefore have an adequate familiarity with and understanding of pertinent law, which should be referred to in their awards when necessary. It is generally held that statutory enactments are paramount, and that direct agreements between the parties should be made in the light of a statute's existence and potential applicability. Even though perhaps authorised to do so under the parties' agreement, an arbitrator should not issue an award that would require one or both of the parties to violate the law. If requested to enforce awards, the courts will obviously examine the situation carefully if breaches of the law may result from compliance with an award ; the courts would in fact hold an award to be illegal if its implementation would infringe any existing law. Arbitrators will generally refrain from interpreting statutes, confining their responsibility to the interpretation of the parties' agreement.

NATURE OF REMEDY

In cases where a grievance is held to be well founded and the arbitrator is empowered to award a remedy, the appropriate measure of relief must be selected. While the agreement may make explicit provision for the remedies applicable in certain cases, it will generally be for the arbitrator to determine what is appropriate, within the limits of the remedy sought by the grievant. In determining the remedy to be awarded the arbitrator will be guided by the general principle that a person whose rights have been infringed is entitled to full redress, so that the grievant's position will ultimately be the same as it would have been if there had been no infringement. In case of unjustified dismissal, for example, the remedy may be reinstatement with payment of lost earnings. In cases of improper distribution of overtime, the remedy might consist of payment of the remuneration that would have been paid if the grievant had been given overtime work in compliance with the terms of the agreement. In some cases the arbitrator may find that a worker committed a breach of discipline, but that the sanction applied by the employer was excessive. In such case a lesser remedy may be provided : for example if a worker was dismissed for a minor first offence the arbitrator may order reinstatement in employment, with no reimbursement of lost earnings, or only partial reimbursement. In general, arbitrators are reluctant to award punitive damages (i.e. damages in excess of those actually suffered, in order to punish the party violating the agreement) unless so authorised by the parties' agreement.

CONTENTS OF THE AWARD

In certain countries it is common practice for the final outcome of arbitration to be a short, written award with a findings of facts and the arbitrator's decision. Under other practice, the arbitrator's final determination is generally a longer document giving not merely the findings but also the reasoning leading up to the decision : it is held that reasoned decisions are necessary in order to explain exactly why the agreement was interpreted as it was, so that the parties will have guidance for their future conduct. Such awards can become a part of the recorded relationship between the parties and be treated as a supplement to the collective agreement. In some cases the parties specifically request the arbitrator to set out recommendations for their future course of conduct or for a procedure to avoid the recurrence of similar problems in the future. Such a written opinion becomes a guide for the future action of the parties. In any event the questions of whether the award should be a written one at all and, if so, of what it should contain are subject to the agreement of the parties, who may decide, in order to avoid delay and additional costs, that the award should be as brief as possible and that the arbitrator need not give the reasons for the decision. The arbitrator will be guided by such agreement or direction of the parties, provided it is made before the hearing closes.

The award may begin with a statement indicating the names of the parties concerned, the listing or documentation number of the grievance, and the date of the decision. It might also set forth at the outset the authority of the arbitrator and the procedural details concerned with the case. For instance, the opening paragraphs might read as follows :

The undersigned arbitrator, designated by the parties pursuant to the terms of Article C of their collective agreement dated 1 December 1975, held a hearing on the company premises on 5 January 1976, at which time the issue set out below was submitted to arbitration.

The Company was represented by John Jones, Counsel, and the Union by Robert Smith, Representative.

A transcript was taken and subsequently distributed to the parties.

The witnesses were the following ...

After this opening statement it is customary to set out the issue that was in dispute, and to indicate whether the statement of the issue had been agreed upon between the parties. It is then appropriate to set out as concisely as possible a statement of the essential background and facts of the case—both those undisputed and those disputed. The provisions of the collective agreement upon which the grievance was based are also given, and possibly excerpts from other relevant documents. The statement usually concludes with information on the circumstances surrounding the lodging of the grievance. Where necessary, the parties' contentions and arguments may be concisely summarised in the next section, beginning with the arguments of the moving party, which are followed by those of the other side. The final section of the award is devoted to the arbitrator's findings and conclusions regarding the points raised, to the decision on the issue submitted to arbitration by the parties, and if desired to the reasons for the decision.

In writing the award, the arbitrator should concentrate on the main issues raised in the case. If the determination on the issues is sufficient to resolve the dispute, the arbitrator may deal with them exclusively, indicating the irrelevance of other, minor issues ; otherwise a decision must be taken on each of the issues. The language used must be clear, so that there is no misunderstanding of the content of the award.

ISSUANCE

The deadline for the issuance of the award may be established by the arbitrator, the parties, the designating agency or the legislature. In general, the arbitrator should endeavour to issue written awards as soon as they are completed, in order to close the files and provide the parties with as expeditious service as possible. When a deadline is specified, it generally runs from the closing of the parties' submission of their respective cases, whether that be at the termination of the hearing or at the time of submission of written briefs. The rules of a designating agency may include specific deadlines for the issuance of awards. The normal period within which awards should be issued should not exceed 30 days from the conclusion of the hearing or the submission of briefs. If the parties themselves have agreed to a time limit, or even under the rules of a designating agency, it is possible for the parties to agree to a waiver of the deadline to enable the arbitrator to have more time to finish writing the award.

In cases of disciplinary dismissal it is essential for the arbitrator to issue the award as soon as possible, even ahead of the prescribed deadline. A worker whose dismissal is maintained, and who has remained idle in the meantime, will thus be able to proceed at once to look for other employment. On the other hand, if the award provides for reinstatement, it will shorten the period during which the worker is unpaid as well as limit the amount of back wages that may have to be paid.

A written award is signed by the arbitrator, and bears the date of its issuance. Where there is a tripartite arbitration board, it is usual for all the members of the board to sign the award, any dissent from the majority view being indicated next to the dissenting member's signature, and a dissenting opinion stating the dissenter's reasons being appended if that member so wishes.

ENFORCEMENT

As has been indicated in Chapter 1, the principal advantages of the system of private arbitration of grievance disputes depend in large part on the fact that the arbitral awards are final and binding upon the parties. In most cases, it can be expected that if the parties have voluntarily agreed to include a provision to this effect in their collective agreement, they will abide by the arbitrator's decision unless it is vitiated by an abuse of authority or manifest partiality. Indeed it is hardly likely that the system will succeed if the parties do not respect these decisions in the great majority of cases. However, there may be cases that arise in which one of the parties refuses to abide by the arbitrator's award. If this occurs, the other party may seek to have the award enforced by the courts. Whether the courts will enforce such awards when so requested may depend upon public policy on the question. This policy may be determined by the courts themselves, if they decide under general contract principles that agreements to submit such disputes to final and binding arbitration are enforceable by the courts, or it may be determined by provisions to this effect in arbitration statutes or labour relations legislation. Where arbitral awards are enforceable by the courts, it may be possible for a recalcitrant party to seek to have an award declared invalid on certain specified grounds, such as abuse of authority, manifest partiality or gross incompetence. [1]

RESPONSIBILITY AND MORAL AUTHORITY OF THE ARBITRATOR

The success of grievance arbitration depends on the commitment of the parties themselves and of the arbitrator they select to achieving a manifestly equitable settlement of grievance disputes. This fact should govern the conduct of arbitrators whenever there may be a temptation to allow certain considerations of expediency to influence the contents of an award.

On some occasions the parties will approach the arbitrator after the close of the hearing but before the issue of the award with a request for a specific award which was not previously mentioned. For example, the company may admit that a claim should be granted, contrary to its professed opposition, expressed only to support a foreman's inappropriate order which the management admits was wrong ; or the union may suggest that a claim that had been put forward for internal union reasons should be denied. In

---

[1] See above, p. 11.

such cases the arbitrators alone, even though they owe their appointment and their power to the parties, have the authority to decide how the grievance in question should be disposed of, and should exercise that authority as they consider appropriate in the light of the collective agreement and the facts of the case. If the award proposed by the parties in a case is contrary to what the arbitrator believes to be appropriate, their pleas should be ignored and the case decided according to the arbitrator's conscience. It may be tempting to accede to the wishes of the parties, particularly since such action might increase a person's future acceptability to them as an arbitrator, but once designated by the parties to decide a case arbitrators are bound by the agreement, their conscience, and their integrity to do what they believe to be right. This is particularly important if a case involves an individual grievant whose rights both sides are willing to compromise to maintain smoother management-union relations. Such an individual may have rights under the agreement, which an arbitrator is under an obligation to protect.

An arbitrator may also be tempted to express opinions on a matter that may be related to the issue in dispute, but is not really material to the resolution of that issue or to the grounds for decision. Because any award will normally disappoint the losing party, and may thus reduce the future acceptability of the arbitrator to that party, the arbitrator may seek to include in the award opinions that will assuage the feelings of the losing party, for example by taking a favourable view of the losing party's position or putting some kind of blame on the other party on a related point. For example, in a disciplinary case, the arbitrator may uphold the management's decision, but implicitly or explicitly put into question the adequacy or justness of an existing policy by adding an opinion to the effect that the trouble would not have arisen had the management acted otherwise. The danger is that apart from unnecessarily prolonging the text of the award, such statements can be a source of trouble for the parties. In the example cited, the union (as the losing party) would be encouraged to demand modification of the management policy in question. The management would probably resist, and the result would be a dispute unwittingly instigated by the arbitrator. More often, however, the practical result of such statements is resentment by the winning party, a result which is contrary to the arbitrator's purpose in making them.

The other danger is that an arbitrator called upon to deal with a series of grievances involving the same two parties may try to issue awards favourable to each alternately. Such conduct will not be regarded by the parties as evidence of an impartiality that will make the arbitrator any more acceptable to them ; indeed it may lead to the opposite result, since the parties will no doubt understand that the arbitrator lacks the courage and integrity to decide each case on its merits. An arbitrator who decides cases with a view to maintaining an over-all labour-management balance is bound to have a short-lived career in arbitration. The parties know their strengths and weaknesses in each case and may even sense victory or loss in presenting their side of it. The arbitrator who hands down a decision contrary to this expectation with a poorly reasoned award will become suspect to both parties.

APPENDICES

1. EXAMINATION OF GRIEVANCES RECOMMENDATION, 1967

The General Conference of the International Labour Organisation,

Having been convened at Geneva by the Governing Body of the International Labour Office, and having met in its Fifty-first Session on 7 June 1967, and

Noting the terms of existing international labour Recommendations dealing with various aspects of labour-management relations, and in particular the Collective Agreements Recommendation, 1951, the Voluntary Conciliation and Arbitration Recommendation, 1951, the Co-operation at the Level of the Undertaking Recommendation, 1952, and the Termination of Employment Recommendation, 1963, and

Considering that additional standards are called for, and

Noting the terms of the Communications within the Undertaking Recommendation, 1967, and

Having decided upon adoption of certain proposals with regard to the examination of grievances within the undertaking, which is included in the fifth item on the agenda of the session, and

Having determined that those proposals shall take the form of a Recommendation,

adopts this twenty-ninth day of June of the year one thousand nine hundred and sixty-seven the following Recommendation, ... :

I. *Methods of Implementation*

1. Effect may be given to this Recommendation through national laws or regulations, collective agreements, works rules, or arbitration awards, or in such other manner consistent with national practice as may be appropriate under national conditions.

II. *General Principles*

2. Any worker who, acting individually or jointly with other workers, considers that he has grounds for a grievance should have the right—

(a) to submit such grievance without suffering any prejudice whatsoever as a result ; and

(b) to have such grievance examined pursuant to an appropriate procedure.

3. The grounds for a grievance may be any measure or situation which concerns the relations between employer and worker or which affects or may affect the conditions of employment of one or several workers in the undertaking when that measure or situation appears contrary to provisions of an applicable collective agreement or of an individual contract of employment, to works rules, to laws or regulations or to the custom or usage of the occupation, branch of economic activity or country, regard being had to principles of good faith.

4. (1) The provisions of this Recommendation are not applicable to collective claims aimed at the modification of terms and conditions of employment.

(2) The determination of the distinction between cases in which a complaint submitted by one or more workers is a grievance to be examined under the procedures provided for in this Recommendation and cases in which a complaint is a general claim to be dealt with by means of collective bargaining or under some other procedure for settlement of disputes is a matter for national law or practice.

5. When procedures for the examination of grievances are established through collective agreements, the parties to such an agreement should be encouraged to include therein a provision to the effect that, during the period of its validity, they undertake to promote settlement of grievances under the procedures provided and to abstain from any action which might impede the effective functioning of these procedures.

6. Workers' organisations or the representatives of the workers in the undertaking should be associated, with equal rights and responsibilities, with the employers or their organisations, preferably by way of agreement, in the establishment and implementation of grievance procedures within the undertaking, in conformity with national law or practice.

7. (1) With a view to minimising the number of grievances, the greatest attention should be given to the establishment and proper functioning of a sound personnel policy, which should take into account and respect the rights and interests of the workers.

(2) In order to achieve such a policy and to solve social questions affecting the workers within the undertaking, management should, before taking a decision, co-operate with the workers' representatives.

8. As far as possible, grievances should be settled within the undertaking itself according to effective procedures which are adapted to the conditions of the country, branch of economic activity and undertaking concerned and which give the parties concerned every assurance of objectivity.

9. None of the provisions of this Recommendation should result in limiting the right of a worker to apply directly to the competent labour authority or to a labour court or other judicial authority in respect of a grievance, where such right is recognised under national laws or regulations.

III. *Procedures within the Undertaking*

10. (1) As a general rule an attempt should initially be made to settle grievances directly between the worker affected, whether assisted or not, and his immediate supervisor.

(2) Where such attempt at settlement has failed or where the grievance is of such a nature that a direct discussion between the worker affected and his immediate supervisor would be inappropriate, the worker should be entitled to have his case considered at one or more higher steps, depending on the nature of the grievance and on the structure and size of the undertaking.

11. Grievance procedures should be so formulated and applied that there is a real possibility of achieving at each step provided for by the procedure a settlement of the case freely accepted by the worker and the employer.

12. Grievance procedures should be as uncomplicated and as rapid as possible, and appropriate time limits may be prescribed if necessary for this purpose ; formality in the application of these procedures should be kept to a minimum.

13. (1) The worker concerned should have the right to participate directly in the grievance procedure and to be assisted or represented during the examination of his grievance by a representative of a workers' organisation, by a representative of the workers in the undertaking, or by any other person of his own choosing, in conformity with national law or practice.

(2) The employer should have the right to be assisted or represented by an employers' organisation.

(3) Any person employed in the same undertaking who assists or represents the worker during the examination of his grievance should, on condition that he acts in conformity with the grievance procedure, enjoy the same protection as that enjoyed by the worker under Paragraph 2, clause *(a)*, of this Recommendation.

14. The worker concerned, or his representative if the latter is employed in the same undertaking, should be allowed sufficient time to participate in the procedure for the examination of the grievance and should not suffer any loss of remuneration because of his absence from work as a result of such participation, account being taken of any rules and practices, including safeguards against abuses, which might be provided for by legislation, collective agreements or other appropriate means.

15. If the parties consider it necessary, minutes of the proceedings may be drawn up in mutual agreement and be available to the parties.

16. (1) Appropriate measures should be taken to ensure that grievance procedures, as well as the rules and practices governing their operation and the conditions for having recourse to them, are brought to the knowledge of the workers.

(2) Any worker who has submitted a grievance should be kept informed of the steps being taken under the procedure and of the action taken on his grievance.

IV. *Adjustment of Unsettled Grievances*

17. Where all efforts to settle the grievance within the undertaking have failed, there should be a possibility, account being taken of the nature of the grievance, for final settlement of such grievance through one or more of the following procedures :

(a) procedures provided for by collective agreement, such as joint examination of the case by the employers' and workers' organisations concerned or voluntary arbitration by a person or persons designated with the agreement of the employer and worker concerned or their respective organisations ;

(b) conciliation or arbitration by the competent public authorities ;

(c) recourse to a labour court or other judicial authority ;

(d) any other procedure which may be appropriate under national conditions.

18. (1) The worker should be allowed the time off necessary to take part in the procedures referred to in Paragraph 17 of this Recommendation.

(2) Recourse by the worker to any of the procedures provided for in Paragraph 17 should not involve for him any loss of remuneration when his grievance is proved justified in the course of these procedures. Every effort should be made, where possible, for the operation of these procedures outside the working hours of the workers concerned.

2. SAMPLE GRIEVANCE PROCEDURE ENDING IN ARBITRATION

1. If a grievance or complaint arises under the terms of the agreement, the aggrieved worker or his trade union representative shall first refer the matter to the worker's immediate supervisor.

2. If the grievance is not satisfactorily settled at that stage, it may be raised with the personnel manager [or other designated representative of management].

3. If the grievance is not then settled, the matter may be referred to the general manager.

[The above procedure will have to be adjusted to the structure of the undertaking concerned. Time limits may be specified for the submission of grievances or appeals and for reply by the employer's representative at each stage.]

4. If any grievance concerning the interpretation or application of this agreement is not satisfactorily settled through the procedure outlined in sections 1 to 3, it may be submitted to arbitration by either party upon written notice to the other party. This notice must be given within 30 days of the final decision of the employer under section 3.

5. The arbitrator shall be selected by a representative of the employer and a representative of the union. If they are unable to agree upon an arbitrator, either party may refer the question of designation to the [name of the designation agency] for processing in accordance with its rules.

6. The decision of the arbitrator shall be final and binding upon the employer, the union and the worker or workers affected.

7. The arbitrator shall have no power to add to, subtract from, or modify any provision of this agreement.

8. The remuneration of the arbitrator and the general expenses of arbitration shall be shared equally between the employer and the union.

3. AMERICAN ARBITRATION ASSOCIATION VOLUNTARY LABOR ARBITRATION RULES

1. *Agreement of parties.* The parties shall be deemed to have made these rules a part of their arbitration agreement whenever, in a collective bargaining agreement or submission, they have provided for arbitration by the American Arbitration Association (hereinafter AAA) or under its rules. These rules shall apply in the form obtaining at the time the arbitration is initiated.

2. *Name of tribunal.* Any tribunal constituted by the parties under these rules shall be called the Voluntary Labor Arbitration Tribunal.

3. *Administrator.* When parties agree to arbitrate under these rules and an arbitration is instituted thereunder, they thereby authorize the AAA to administer the arbitration. The authority and obligations of the administrator are as provided in the agreement of the parties and in these rules.

4. *Delegation of duties.* The duties of the AAA may be carried out through such representatives or committees as the AAA may direct.

5. *National panel of labor arbitrators.* The AAA shall establish and maintain a national panel of labor arbitrators and shall appoint arbitrators therefrom, as hereinafter provided.

6. *Office of Tribunal.* The general office of the Labor Arbitration Tribunal is the headquarters of the AAA, which may, however, assign the administration of an arbitration to any of its regional offices.

7. *Initiation under an arbitration clause in a collective bargaining agreement.* Arbitration under an arbitration clause in a collective bargaining agreement under these rules may be initiated by either party in the following manner :

(a) by giving written notice to the other party of intention to arbitrate (demand), which notice shall contain a statement setting forth the nature of the dispute and the remedy sought ; and

(b) by filing at any regional office of the AAA two copies of said notice, together with a copy of the collective bargaining agreement, or such parts thereof as relate to the dispute, including the arbitration provisions ; after the arbitrator is appointed, no new or different claim may be submitted to him except with the consent of the arbitrator and all other parties.

8. *Answer.* The party upon whom the demand for arbitration is made may file an answering statement with the AAA within 7 days after notice from the AAA, in which event he shall simultaneously send a copy of his answer to the other party. If no answer is filed within the stated time, it will be assumed that the claim is denied. Failure to file an answer shall not operate to delay the arbitration.

9. *Initiation under a submission.* Parties to any collective bargaining agreement may initiate an arbitration under these rules by filing at any regional office of the AAA two copies of a written agreement to arbitrate under these rules (submission), signed by the parties and setting forth the nature of the dispute and the remedy sought.

10. *Fixing of locale.* The parties may mutually agree upon the locale where the arbitration is to be held. If the locale is not designated in the collective bargaining agreement or submission, and if there is a dispute as to the appropriate locale, the AAA shall have the power to determine the locale and its decision shall be binding.

11. *Qualifications of arbitrator.* No person shall serve as a neutral arbitrator in any arbitration in which he has any financial or personal interest in the result of the arbitration, unless the parties, in writing, waive such disqualification.

12. *Appointment from panel.* If the parties have not appointed an arbitrator and have not provided any other method of appointment, the arbitrator shall be appointed in the following manner : Immediately after the filing of the demand or submission, the AAA shall submit simultaneously to each party an identical list of names of persons chosen from the labor panel. Each party shall have 7 days from the mailing date in which to cross off any names to which he objects, number the remaining names indicating the order of his preference, and return the list to the AAA. If a party does not return the list within the time specified, all persons named therein shall be deemed acceptable. From among the persons who have been approved on both lists, and in accordance with the designated order of mutual preference, the AAA shall invite the acceptance of an arbitrator to serve. If the parties fail to agree upon any of the persons named or if those named decline or are unable to act, or if for any other reason the appointment cannot be made from the submitted lists, the administrator shall have power to make the appointment from other members of the panel without the submission of any additional lists.

13. *Direct appointment by parties.* If the agreement of the parties names an arbitrator or specifies a method of appointing an arbitrator, that designation or

method shall be followed. The notice of appointment, with the name and address of such arbitrator, shall be filed with the AAA by the appointing party.

If the agreement specifies a period of time within which an arbitrator shall be appointed, and any party fails to make such appointment within that period, the AAA may make the appointment.

If no period of time is specified in the agreement, the AAA shall notify the parties to make the appointment and if within 7 days thereafter such arbitrator has not been so appointed, the AAA shall make the appointment.

14. *Appointment of neutral arbitrator by party-appointed arbitrators.* If the parties have appointed their arbitrators, or if either or both of them have been appointed as provided in section 13, and have authorized such arbitrators to appoint a neutral arbitrator within a specified time and no appointment is made within such time or any agreed extension thereof, the AAA may appoint a neutral arbitrator, who shall act as chairman.

If no period of time is specified for appointment of the neutral arbitrator and the parties do not make the appointment within 7 days from the date of the appointment of the last party-appointed arbitrator, the AAA shall appoint such neutral arbitrator, who shall act as chairman.

If the parties have agreed that the arbitrators shall appoint the neutral arbitrator from the panel, the AAA shall furnish to the party-appointed arbitrators, in the manner prescribed in section 12, a list selected from the panel, and the appointment of the neutral arbitrator shall be made as prescribed in such section.

15. *Number of arbitrators.* If the arbitration agreement does not specify the number of arbitrators, the dispute shall be heard and determined by one arbitrator, unless the parties otherwise agree.

16. *Notice to arbitrator of his appointment.* Notice of the appointment of the neutral arbitrator shall be mailed to the arbitrator by the AAA and the signed acceptance of the arbitrator shall be filed with the AAA prior to the opening of the first hearing.

17. *Disclosure by arbitrator of disqualification.* Prior to accepting his appointment, the prospective neutral arbitrator shall disclose any circumstances likely to create a presumption of bias or which he believes might disqualify him as an impartial arbitrator. Upon receipt of such information, the AAA shall immediately disclose it to the parties. If either party declines to waive the presumptive disqualification, the vacancy thus created shall be filled in accordance with the applicable provisions of these rules.

18. *Vacancies.* If any arbitrator should resign, die, withdraw, refuse or be unable or disqualified to perform the duties of his office, the AAA shall, on proof satisfactory to it, declare the office vacant. Vacancies shall be filled in the same manner as that governing the making of the original appointment, and the matter shall be reheard by the new arbitrator.

19. *Time and place of hearing.* The arbitrator shall fix the time and place for each hearing. At least 5 days prior thereto the AAA shall mail notice of the time and place of hearing to each party, unless the parties otherwise agree.

20. *Representation by counsel.* Any party may be represented at the hearing by counsel or by other authorized representative.

21. *Stenographic record.* The AAA will make the necessary arrangements for the taking of an official stenographic record of the testimony whenever such record is requested by one or more parties. The requesting party or parties shall pay the cost of such record directly to the reporting agency in accordance with their agreement.

22. *Attendance at hearings.* Persons having a direct interest in the arbitration are entitled to attend hearings. The arbitrator shall have the power to require the retirement of any witness or witnesses during the testimony of other witnesses. It shall be discretionary with the arbitrator to determine the propriety of the attendance of any other persons.

23. *Adjournments.* The arbitrator for good cause shown may adjourn the hearing upon the request of a party or upon his own initiative, and shall adjourn when all the parties agree thereto.

24. *Oaths.* Before proceeding with the first hearing, each arbitrator may take an oath of office, and if required by law, shall do so. The arbitrator may, in his discretion, require witnesses to testify under oath administered by any duly qualified person, and if required by law or requested by either party, shall do so.

25. *Majority decision.* Whenever there is more than one arbitrator, all decisions of the arbitrators shall be by majority vote. The award shall also be made by majority vote unless the concurrence of all is expressly required.

26. *Order of proceedings.* A hearing shall be opened by the filing of the oath of the arbitrator, where required, and by the recording of the place, time and date of hearing, the presence of the arbitrator and parties, and counsel if any, and the receipt by the arbitrator of the demand and answer, if any, or the submission.

Exhibits, when offered by either party, may be received in evidence by the arbitrator. The names and addresses of all witnesses and exhibits in order received shall be made a part of the record.

The arbitrator may, in his discretion, vary the normal procedure under which the initiating party first presents his claim, but in any case shall afford full and equal opportunity to all parties for presentation of relevant proofs.

27. *Arbitration in the absence of a party.* Unless the law provides to the contrary the arbitration may proceed in the absence of any party, who, after due notice, fails to be present or fails to obtain an adjournment. An award shall not be made solely on the default of a party. The arbitrator shall require the other party to submit such evidence as he may require for the making of an award.

28. *Evidence.* The parties may offer such evidence as they desire and shall produce such additional evidence as the arbitrator may deem necessary to an understanding and determination of the dispute. When the arbitrator is authorized by law to subpoena witnesses and documents, he may do so upon his own initiative or upon the request of any party. The arbitrator shall be the judge of the relevancy and materiality of the evidence offered and conformity to legal rules of evidence shall not be necessary. All evidence shall be taken in the presence of all of the arbitrators and all of the parties except where any of the parties is absent in default or has waived his right to be present.

29. *Evidence by affidavit and filing of documents.* The arbitrator may receive and consider the evidence of witnesses by affidavit, but shall give it only such weight as he deems proper after consideration of any objections made to its admission.

All documents not filed with the arbitrator at the hearing but which are arranged at the hearing or subsequently by agreement of the parties to be submitted, shall be filed with the AAA for transmission to the arbitrator. All parties shall be afforded opportunity to examine such documents.

30. *Inspection.* Whenever the arbitrator deems it necessary, he may make an inspection in connection with the subject matter of the dispute after written notice to the parties who may, if they so desire, be present at such inspection.

31. *Closing of hearings.* The arbitrator shall inquire of all parties whether they have any further proofs to offer or witnesses to be heard. Upon receiving negative replies, the arbitrator shall declare the hearings closed and a minute thereof shall be recorded. If briefs or other documents are to be filed, the hearings shall be declared closed as of the final date set by the arbitrator for filing with the AAA. The time limit within which the arbitrator is required to make his award shall commence to run, in the absence of other agreement by the parties, upon the closing of the hearings.

32. *Reopening of hearings.* The hearings may be reopened by the arbitrator on his own motion, or on the motion of either party, for good cause shown, at any time before the award is made, but if the reopening of the hearing would prevent the making of the award within the specific time agreed upon by the parties in the contract out of which the controversy has arisen, the matter may not be reopened, unless both parties agree upon the extension of such time limit. When no specific date is fixed in the contract, the arbitrator may reopen the hearings, and the arbitrator shall have 30 days from the closing of the reopened hearings within which to make an award.

33. *Waiver of rules.* Any party who proceeds with the arbitration after knowledge that any provision or requirement of these rules has not been complied with and who fails to state his objection thereto in writing, shall be deemed to have waived his right to object.

34. *Waiver of oral hearing.* The parties may provide, by written agreement, for the waiver of oral hearings. If the parties are unable to agree as to the procedure, the AAA shall specify a fair and equitable procedure.

35. *Extensions of time.* The parties may modify any period of time by mutual agreement. The AAA for good cause may extend any period of time established by these rules, except the time for making the award. The AAA shall notify the parties of any such extension of time and its reason therefor.

36. *Serving of notices.* Each party to a submission or other agreement which provides for arbitration under these rules shall be deemed to have consented and shall consent that any papers, notices or process necessary or proper for the initiation or continuation of an arbitration under these rules and for any court action in connection therewith or the entry of judgement on an award made thereunder, may be served upon such party *(a)* by mail addressed to such party or his attorney at his last known address, or *(b)* by personal service, within or without the state wherein the arbitration is to be held.

37. *Time of award.* The award shall be rendered promptly by the arbitrator and, unless otherwise agreed by the parties, or specified by the law, not later than 30 days from the date of closing the hearings, or if oral hearings have been waived, then from the date of transmitting the final statements and proofs to the arbitrator.

38. *Form of award.* The award shall be in writing and shall be signed either by the neutral arbitrator or by a concurring majority if there be more than one arbitrator. The parties shall advise the AAA whenever they do not require the arbitrator to accompany the award with an opinion.

39. *Award upon settlement.* If the parties settle their dispute during the course of the arbitration, the arbitrator, upon their request, may set forth the terms of the agreed settlement in an award.

40. *Delivery of award to parties.* Parties shall accept as legal delivery of the award the placing of the award or a true copy thereof in the mail by the AAA, addressed to such party at his last known address or to his attorney, or personal

service of the award, or the filing of the award in any manner which may be prescribed by law.

41. *Release of documents for judicial proceedings.* The AAA shall, upon the written request of a party, furnish to such party at his expense certified facsimiles of any papers in the AAA's possession that may be required in judicial proceedings relating to the arbitration.

42. *Judicial proceedings.* The AAA is not a necessary party in judicial proceedings relating to the arbitration.

43. *Administrative fee.* As a non-profit organization, the AAA shall prescribe an administrative fee schedule to compensate it for the cost of providing administrative services. The schedule in effect at the time of filing shall be applicable.

44. *Expenses.* The expenses of witnesses for either side shall be paid by the party producing such witnesses.

Expenses of the arbitration, other than the cost of the stenographic record, including required traveling and other expenses of the arbitrator and of AAA representatives, and the expenses of any witnesses or the cost of any proofs produced at the direct request of the arbitrator, shall be borne equally by the parties unless they agree otherwise, or unless the arbitrator in his award assesses such expenses or any part thereof against any specified party or parties.

45. *Communication with arbitrator.* There shall be no communication between the parties and a neutral arbitrator other than at oral hearings. Any other oral or written communications from the parties to the arbitrator shall be directed to the AAA for transmittal to the arbitrator.

46. *Interpretation and application of rules.* The arbitrator shall interpret and apply these rules in so far as they relate to his power and duties. When there is more than one arbitrator and a difference arises among them concerning the meaning or application of any such rules, it shall be decided by majority vote. If that is unobtainable, either arbitrator or party may refer the question to the AAA for final decision. All other rules shall be interpreted and applied by the AAA.

72

137 8 551